Parental
Death and
Psychological
Development

Parental Death and Psychological Development

SCHOOL OF
CALIFORNIA PROFESSIONAL
PSYCHOLOGY
LOS ANGELES

Ellen B. Berlinsky
Counseling and Family
Services, Inc.

Henry B. Biller
University of Rhode Island

LexingtonBooks
D.C. Heath and Company
Lexington, Massachusetts
Toronto

Library of Congress Cataloging in Publication Data

Berlinsky, Ellen B.
  Parental death and psychological development.

  Includes bibliographical references and index.
  1. Children and death.   2. Parental deprivation.   3. Bereavement—
Psychological aspects.   I. Biller, Henry B.   II. Title.
[DNLM: 1. Maternal deprivation.   2. Paternal
deprivation.   3. Child development.   WS 105.5.D5   B515p]
BF723.D3B47   1982   155.9′37   82–48015
ISBN 0–669–05875–0

Published simultaneously in Canada

Printed in the United States of America

International Standard Book Number: 0–669–05875–0

Library of Congress Catalog Card Number: 82–48015

To
Gary Schine
and
Maggie Salter

Contents

Figures and Tables

Preface

From our clinical and research endeavors, we have been impressed with the immediate and the long-term influence of parental separation and loss on children and their families. One of the authors had been particularly struck by the incidence of parental death in the backgrounds she has dealt with in her clinical work. This topic has special significance for the other author because of the death of both his father and grandfather when he was a child, and his mother when he was a young adult. The authors were fortunate that they had the opportunity to work together in two different settings: an outpatient service in a community mental-health center and a psychology department in a university.

A number of people deserve thanks for their assistance in the preparation of this book. Three individuals at the University of Rhode Island were extremely helpful: Marge Bumpus, Ira Gross, and Peter Merenda made distinct contributions to the conceptualization and implementation of this project.

1   Introduction

The loss of a parent through death is an experience that has touched and will continue to touch the lives of thousands of children in this country. In 1978, 3.5 percent of the under-eighteen-year-old population had, at some point during childhood, lost a father through death. In the same year, 1.4 percent of the child population had been affected by the death of a mother (U.S. Social Security Administration 1979). What this experience means in terms of the affected children's future lives has been the source of a great deal of speculation and research. It has been the concern of parents who anticipate, or have undergone, the loss of a spouse, and of professionals who deal with bereaved children. Such concerned adults wonder how best to treat parentally bereaved children and how to minimize the anticipated negative consequences of the death of a parent. For researchers, the general question has been how the death of a parent affects a child's future adjustment and development, and whether these children do, in fact, differ from those in families in which a parent has not died. Preliminary answers to these concerns, derived from popular wisdom as well as from research, have influenced beliefs about and treatment of children who have lost a parent through death.

There is an assumption among mental-health practitioners as well as the general public that experiencing the death of a parent during childhood inevitably influences an individual's future adjustment and development, and that the effects are negative. Attempts have been made to test this assumption, but the validity of research efforts is in question. A survey of the varied literature on the subject has not revealed the existence of a source that systematically summarizes and critiques the research. There has been no comprehensive review that establishes whether, in fact, those who have lost a parent do differ from those who have not had this experience. The implications of the prevalence of this unverified assumption are extensive. Accepted views on the consequences of early parent-death may well influence the expectations and behaviors of others with regard to bereaved children. Decisions about educational and therapeutic programs may be made on the basis of such expectations. It is possible that these changes in the treatment of children who have lost a parent through death—and not the actual parent loss—may affect behavior. Long- or short-term depression might be expected, for example,

1

and concerned adults could consequently insist on the expression of emotions consistent with depression. Children who are not depressed but are treated in this way could well develop feelings of guilt and negative self-worth that are, in fact, symptoms of depression.

A preliminary step in exploring the adjustment and development of children subsequent to a parent's death is an examination of the characteristics of such an experience. Loss of a parent occurs within a personal, family, and social context, and differences in variables at each level would be expected to affect the way in which an individual reacts. Such factors as the way in which the death occurs (sudden or prolonged illness, suicide, homicide, war, or accident); the parent's attitude toward his/her death, age, sex, and relationship with the child; the child's preparation for, and involvement in the mourning process; and changes in the behavior and expectations of others, in family structure, income level, and residence need to be considered in any analysis of a child's subsequent behaviors. Family characteristics before and after the death, such as family relationships and adjustments, family structure (number, sexes and ordinal position of children, and presence of extended-family members), socioeconomic status, cultural background and ethnicity, and religious- and ethical-belief system also need to be taken into account. Finally, consideration must be given to prior and subsequent child-specific variables such as age, sex, temperament, cognitive state of development, understanding of the concept of death, academic achievement and status, creativity and special abilities or disabilities, physical development and health, personality, affective adjustment, and social behavior. A schematic representation of this process is shown in figure 1–1.

In studying the conditions and behaviors that follow a parent's death, it would seem important to consider these antecedent and process variables. To treat persons who have lost a parent as a homogeneous group is to ignore complexities of the experience that have been shown to influence outcome (Biller 1971, 1974, 1981). One example of a study that demonstrates the involvement of multiple variables on children's behavior subsequent to a parent's death is that of Shepherd and Barraclough (1976). These investigators, using a longitudinal format, showed that reactions of children to a parent's suicide varied widely although, as a group, they functioned less adequately in socio-emotional behavior than did controls. Those whose behavior was judged to be disturbed were more likely to have had parents who had had marital problems, involvement in criminal activity, or emotional difficulties. The disturbed children were also more likely to have changed residences after their parent's death. Clearly, had the researchers examined the subsequent behavior of

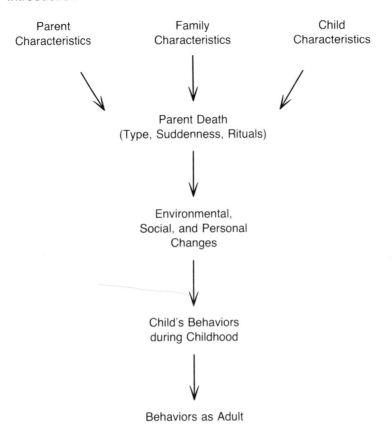

| Parent Characteristics | Family Characteristics | Child Characteristics |

Parent Death
(Type, Suddenness, Rituals)

Environmental,
Social, and Personal
Changes

Child's Behaviors
during Childhood

Behaviors as Adult

Figure 1–1. Preliminary General Model of Factors Influencing Development and Adjustment Subsequent to a Parent's Death

the bereaved subjects without investigating background data and later changes in the environment, the resulting information—that children of suicide victims displayed disturbed behavior—would have been misleading. Unfortunately, the studies that have been conducted in this area have varied widely with respect to the degree to which they account for, and attempt to analyze the significance of variables specific to the child and his/her environment beyond the absence of a parent due to death.

Studies on the conditions and behaviors following the death of a parent have been numerous and diverse in content and scope. There are differences between people who have had a parent die during childhood and those whose childhoods have not been marked by such an experience with respect to psychopathology, personality, juvenile delinquency, criminal behavior, sex role and sexual behavior, marital adjustment, academic and cognitive performance, creativity and genius. Table 1–1 provides a list of studies, theoretical articles, and literature reviews on behaviors and conditions occurring subsequent to a parent's death differentiated by topic.

Most of these studies have investigated the extent to which problems or deficiencies are associated with the death of a parent. It can be speculated that the emphasis on research exploring the extent of negative outcomes is due primarily to the expectations of researchers in this regard. Consideration of the possibility that losing a parent through death during childhood may be associated with positive consequences is not popular. Such a finding would seem to deny much of what is now believed about child development. Research into family relationships might well produce data showing that a child is better off after the death of a physically or sexually abusive parent, for example.

A conceptualization different from that held by many researchers in the field would allow for the possibility that a parent's death could be related to either favorable or adverse consequences. A parent's death could, for example, lead a child to feel deprived and to search throughout his/her life for someone to take responsibility for and care for him or her. The sympathetic behaviors and expectations of others towards the child could well encourage such behaviors and attitudes which, in their most serious form, would be associated with chronic depression. On the other hand, a child who has lost a parent may have the same feelings of affective deprivation and yet channel them differently. She/he may come to feel that she/he must be self reliant and that she/he can expect from life nothing for which she/he does not work. Such an individual could become an energetic achiever whose attitudes and behaviors differ significantly from those of the person who becomes chronically depressed after a parent's death.

Background and process variables specific to the child and his/her environment would be associated with the hypothetical differences in outcome previously described. Also needing investigation are areas of functioning that have been neglected by researchers in the field and that could substantiate or cast doubt upon the proposed conceptualization. Some studies have been conducted to examine the possible association between death of a parent and creativity (Albert 1971; Eisenstadt 1978; Hilgard et al. 1960; and Martindale 1972). Other areas of interest would be career choices and patterns, parenting behavior, the development of special skills and talents as well as the more positive or neutral aspects of affective issues which have not been fully explored. Maturity, assertiveness, and extroversion/introversion are examples of the latter.

The purpose of this book is to organize the existing literature on the

Table 1-1
Research on Behaviors and Conditions Occurring Subsequent to a Parent's Death, by Topic

Emotional Disturbance
Abrahams and Whitlock (1969)
Adam (1973)
Archibald, et al. (1962)
Barry and Lindemann (1960)
Beck, Sethi, and Tuthill (1963)
Bendicksen and Fulton (1975)
Birtchnell (1966)
Birtchnell (1970a)
Birtchnell (1970b)
Birtchnell (1972)
Birtchnell (1975)
Brill and Liston (1966)
Brown (1961)
Brown (1966)
Brown and Harris (1978)
Brown, Harris, and Copeland (1977)
Cain and Fast (1965)
Caplan and Douglas (1969)
Crook and Eliot (1980)
Crook and Raskin (1975)
Dennehy (1966)
Dietrich (1979)
Dorpat (1972)
Earle and Earle (1959)
Epstein et al. (1975)
Felner et al. (1975)
Forest, Fraser, and Priest (1965)
Gay and Tonge (1967)
Granville-Grossman (1966)
Greer (1964)
Greer (1966)
Gregory (1958)
Gregory (1966)
Heckel (1963)
Herzog and Sudia (1973)
Hilgard and Newman (1963)
Hill (1969)
Hill and Price (1969)
Hopkinson and Reed (1966)
Huttunen and Niskanen (1978)
Ilan (1973)
Jacobson, Fasman, and DiMascio (1975)
Kirkpatrick et al. (1965)
Krupp (1972)
Lester and Beck (1976)
Martindale (1972)
Moriarty (1967)
Munro (1966)
Munro and Griffiths (1968)
Nagaraja (1977)
Pitts et al. (1965)
Roy (1978)

Roy (1979)
Seligman and Glesser (1974)
Sethi (1964)
Trunnell (1968)
Tuckman and Regan (1966)
Walton (1958)
Warren (1972)
Wilson, Alltop, and Buffaloe (1967)

Personality
Baggett (1967)
Biller (1971)
Biller (1972)
Birtchnell (1975)
Bluestein (1978)
Haworth (1964)
Hetherington (1972)
Hetherington and Parke (1979)
Illsley and Thompson (1961)
Parish and Copeland (1980)
Santrock and Wohlford (1970)

Immediate Reactions
Cain and Fast (1965)
Freud (1957)
Freud (1961)
Furman (1964)
Furman (1973)
Goldberg (1973)
Kirkpatrick et al. (1965)
Krupp (1972)
Lindemann (1944)
Moss and Moss (1973)
Nagaraja (1977)
Paul and Grosser (1965)
Rudestam (1977)
Silverman and Englander (1975)

Juvenile Delinquency and Criminal Behavior
Brown (1961)
Brown and Eppos (1966)
Earle and Earle (1959)
Epstein et al. (1975)
Fulton and Markusen (1971)
Glueck and Glueck (1950)
Herzog and Sudia (1973)
Huttenan and Niskanen (1978)
Koller (1970)
Monahan (1957)

Sex Role and Sexual Behavior
Archibald et al. (1962)

Table 1–1 Continued

Biller (1971)
Clarke (1961)
Herzog and Sudia (1973)
Hetherington (1972)
Hetherington and Deur (1971)
Lamb and Lamb (1976)
Martindale (1972)
Moran and Abe (1969)

Marital Adjustment
Biller (1971)
Earle and Earle (1959)
Fulton and Markusen (1971)
Gay and Tonge (1967)
Jacobson and Ryder (1969)

Creativity and Genius
Albert (1971)
Cox (1926)
Eisenstadt (1978)
Hilgard, Newman, and Fisk (1960)
Martindale (1972)
Roe (1953)

Academic and Cognitive Performance
Biller (1971)
Herzog and Sudia (1973)
Hetherington and Deur (1971)
Kirkpatrick et al. (1965)
Lifshitz (1976)
Santrock (1972)
Shinn (1976)

child's adjustment and development following the death of a parent in order: (1) to determine whether or not there are immediate or long-term differences between individuals who experience the death of a parent during childhood and those who do not, and, if differences exist, utilizing a multidimensional framework, to identify the nature and sources of these differences, and (2) to develop a conceptual model for studying and understanding individuals undergoing or having undergone the experience. Parental death is viewed within the general context of loss and separation, and comparison of its effects will be made with those of other forms of parental absence, such as divorce. Primary emphasis will be on work relating to children who lose one parent and who are raised within a family context. (Studies of orphans and children raised in institutions will not be a major focus). Material on the correlates of parent death and related subjects, such as the development of the concept of death in children and prevention and treatment programs will be gathered, and analyzed. Empirical studies will be evaluated as to their methodological adequacy, and findings from acceptable studies will be examined in relation to explanations proposed by theorists. An attempt will be made to synthesize relevant information and to identify problems and gaps in the literature. Finally, there will be a discussion of findings and their implications for further research, prevention, and treatment.

2 Methodology

A major task involved in analyzing the literature on the child's adjustment and development following the death of a parent is evaluation of the methodological adequacy of the studies that have been conducted. Clearly, conclusions about the correlates and consequences of experiencing the early loss of a parent through death can be drawn only from studies meeting certain minimum procedural and statistical standards. The purpose of this section is (1) to identify and describe the methodological flaws characteristic of some of the research in the field, and (2) to present the model for evaluating this research constructed for use in the critical analysis currently being undertaken. The model will be utilized in critically analyzing the research. Other procedural aspects of this project will also be explained.

Methodological Issues

The many reviewers of literature in the area of early parental-bereavement have identified a number of aspects of the research that lead to questions about the validity and generalizability of results of the data gathered. At the most general level, Epstein et al. (1975) noted that much of the literature is "case historical and theoretical in nature and scope" (p. 537). When research in any area of inquiry begins with observations on narrow samples, and with hypothesized explanations in order to understand what has been observed, such work is limited in its generalizability. With the exception of the studies concerned with immediate reactions to death, researchers seem to have recognized the need to progress beyond these limitations and a great deal of empirical activity has been generated, particularly over the last twenty years. Unfortunately, this empirical orientation has led to some research that, due to flawed methodology, is as limited in its generalizability as is work based on case studies.

A major problem characteristic of many studies has been the tendency to treat those who have lost a parent through death during childhood as if they were a homogeneous group (Biller 1971, 1974, 1981; Gregory 1958; Herzog and Sudia 1973). Samples have tended to be poorly defined, without consideration of socioeconomic status, temperament, family structure, sex or age at the time of the parental loss and at assessment

7

(Biller 1971, 1974, 1981; Epstein et al. 1975; Shinn 1976). All of these variables are related to differences in behavior, and therefore they need to be accounted for in any interpretation of results. In view of the body of theoretical literature related to age-specific-affective needs of children in their relationships with parents (for example, Bowlby 1960), the failure to account for age at the time of a parent's death, which may result in the grouping of individuals having lost a parent in infancy and in adolescence is particularly surprising. Similarly, the research showing the differential behavior towards and effects of parents on their sons and daughters (Johnson 1963) would point to the importance of specifying and accounting for the sex of both the subject and the deceased parent. Nevertheless, numerous studies not only fail to match subjects on age, sex, and other relevant variables mentioned above, but also fail to provide information on them for use in interpreting results.

Individuals who have lost a parent also differ in the characteristics of the loss experience and the changes that take place in their lives subsequent to the loss. The difficulty in interpreting data resulting from research in which subjects who have experienced various types of parental losses and separations has been pointed out by numerous reviewers (Biller 1971, 1974, 1981; Herzog and Sudia 1973; Shinn 1976). As Shinn has noted, different types of parent loss can represent quite dissimilar affective experiences. Loss through death may be traumatic but is usually not socially stigmatized while a child who loses a parent through divorce, separation, illegitimacy, or desertion, may face personal and family trauma and the negative reactions of others due to social stigma. The way in which a parent's death occurred: through suicide, homicide, war, accident, or sudden or prolonged illness, may also have quite disparate effects on surviving children. The reactions of other family members also may be expected to differ by reason for loss. The attitude and behavior of the remaining parent towards the former spouse and children is apt to vary significantly according to the reason for the loss. These reactions, in turn, would undoubtedly affect their children's behavior. Thus, to consider childhood loss of a parent a single dimension by which to group subjects is a practice that could affect research outcomes to a considerable extent.

Characteristics of the deceased parent may also be related to the subsequent adjustment and development of their children. Sex of the parent who dies may affect the type and degree of behavior change seen in children. As mothers and fathers typically play different roles and fill different needs in the lives of their children, loss of a mother or a father would not be expected to have identical outcomes. Many studies ignore this probability, however, and treat children of deceased parents as a homogeneous group (Hilgard and Newman 1963).

Even less frequently accounted for has been the nature of the relationship the child and parent have had. While an inherent assumption of much research has been that loss of a parent will be a negative experience to be worked through, Hetherington and Deur (1971) have suggested that a parent's absence could be positive if he/she was a major source of conflict in the family. Accounting for the prior relationship of the child and his/her now-deceased parent, therefore, would be important to any interpretations made of research findings.

Changes in the family-living situation occurring after the death of a parent have great potential for contributing to the child's future adjustment and development. These changes may be directly or indirectly related to the loss, or related only in time sequence. It is the view of many researchers that these changes have as much if not more relevance to the child's subsequent behavior as the parent's death does (Biller 1971, 1974, 1981; Hamilton 1977; Herzog and Sudia 1973; Hetherington and Deur 1971; Pedersen 1976; Shinn 1976). Among the family circumstances that may be altered following a parent's death are socioeconomic status, emotional and physical availability of the remaining parent due to increased responsibilities, stress level within the family, employment status of the remaining parent, functional roles played by other family members (siblings, grandparents, other extended family), and the introduction of parent substitutes either as new spouse for the remaining parent or paid caretaker for the children and home. Research in which there is matching on or accounting for these variables shows that they do indeed make a difference to the child's subsequent functioning, as will be shown. It is therefore unfortunate that most studies ignore differences in subjects on these variables.

Other aspects of sample selection have also been criticized by researchers in the field. Epstein et al. (1975), Hilgard and Newman (1963), and Shinn (1976) argued that samples in many studies are too small and too restricted to lead to meaningful conclusions. They presented the overuse of clinic, psychiatric hospital, and other emotionally disturbed or behaviorally disordered populations, with subsequent generalizations to wider groups as a major problem in the research accumulated to date. Findings from such samples would be naturally biased toward results showing some form of maladjustment in subjects, whether normal or disturbed subjects are used as comparison groups. The problem becomes quite serious when unwarranted generalizations to other groups are made. Even if researchers had refrained from such practices, studies of more representative populations would be called for so that a more balanced view of individuals whose childhood experiences have included the death of a parent would be reflected. In order to fully understand the effects of a parent's death, the reactions of subjects showing a variety of characteristics prior to the death (superior, average, and deficient intelligence, and academic performance, emotional disturbance and adequate adjustment) must be assessed.

Closely related to the issue of sample selection and makeup are the presence and characteristics of comparison groups. The use of comparison groups is basic to scientific research as a means of putting findings into perspective. Outcomes become much more meaningful when differences between a group having undergone a specific treatment or possessing specific characteristics (as having lost a parent during childhood) and groups similar except on these variables can be shown. If matching on all variables but the ones being examined is carried out, and significant differences between the groups can be demonstrated, attribution of the differences to the treatment or special group characteristic can be made with a fair degree of certainty.

Much of the more recent research on the correlates of parent death during childhood utilizes comparison groups of some sort. Those that do not, some of which are case histories rather than empirically oriented studies, must be viewed as descriptive accounts providing hypotheses for further investigation. Where generalizations beyond the specific sample are made, without the benefit of a comparison group, conclusions must be questioned.

A more prevalent problem in the literature is the failure to equate groups on significant variables so that valid comparisons can be made. Ideally, matching of groups should be done on all of the variables discussed other than parent death during childhood. If matching is not carried out, differences between groups would be expected on several variables. In a sample of children, for example, those whose parents have died would be expected to be older than the others since their parents would be older (Granville-Grossman 1968; Hilgard and Newman 1963). (Older people are more likely to die.) As other changes in behavior are related to age, matching would prove important. Similarly, those who have lost a parent, particularly a father, are more likely to be of low socioeconomic status and to be a minority-group member before the death. Decreases in family income level also frequently follow a parent's death. These characteristics, too, are related to differences in functioning in a number of areas, and therefore need to be considered in selection of subjects for comparison groups (Biller 1971, 1974, 1981; Epstein et al., 1975; Gregory 1958, 1966; Shinn 1976).

Some researchers have utilized census or life-insurance-table statistics on normal bereavement rates rather than selecting actual subjects as controls. Two difficulties have been characteristic of this procedure. One has been the failure to adjust for secular trends in bereavement. The proportion of children experiencing the death of a parent has decreased since 1910

(Hilgard and Newman 1963), and, at least with fathers, especially since 1940 (Herzog and Sudia 1973). Comparisons have often not reflected these changes. The other problem has been the practice of comparing subjects with groups that are dissimilar on some of the demographic data discussed above.

A problem specific to research on emotionally disturbed populations has been in identifying appropriate groups with which to compare these subjects. A number of studies have compared psychiatric inpatients assigned different diagnoses with one another. Such a procedure presents major difficulties in interpretation due to the lack of specificity regarding diagnostic criteria. If it were assumed that one of the major psychiatric classification systems were used, the validity and reliability of the distinctions made (Quay 1979) could be affected to a large extent. Also, knowledge of a childhood marked by the death of a parent could well affect assignment of the diagnosis, as depression is often expected of individuals with such histories. Since gathering of family background data is a typical prerequisite to psychiatric diagnosis, classification of persons having lost a parent during childhood could be affected to a large extent. Therefore it would be difficult to determine in what ways the groups being compared are similar and different. Also, if no differences in rates of childhood bereavement of parents were found between groups, the possible association between emotional disturbance and parent loss could not be determined. Utilizing ''normal'' subjects would not resolve the problem, however, as major differences in the environments of those who are hospitalized and those who are not would exist. Such factors as restriction of mobility and the ability to determine the course of one's day, lack of privacy, assumption of the patient role, and anxiety about treatment procedures and the outcome of one's illness could all affect an individual's attitudes and behaviors, and therefore research outcomes.

Studies comparing medical hospital patients with psychiatric inpatients would seem to come closer to meeting the requirements for adequate controls. Both groups of subjects would be similar on environmental variables, which might affect responses. However, this procedure has been criticized by Dennehy (1966) who asserted that general-hospital patients are not adequate controls, since studies have shown that a large proportion of such individuals have nonorganic psychiatric disorders.

There would appear to be several reasonable methods of addressing problems in matching emotionally disturbed subjects with controls. If the characteristics of the emotional disturbances of inpatients were operationally defined, different groups of patients could be distinguished and compared. Self report or psychometrist-administered diagnostic instruments or observation and rating systems of proven reliability could be utilized to assess patients' characteristics. The same instruments could be used to screen medical-hospital patients to determine whether they show signs of emotional disturbance and therefore would be inadequate controls. Munro's procedure (1966) of screening medical-hospital controls on the basis of reported histories of affective disorders was one attempt to select appropriate controls for psychiatric patients. Use of a well-tested assessment tool would have improved upon his technique. Whether psychiatric or medical hospital patients are employed as controls, the additional use of a nonhospital control group or comparison of findings with normal bereavement rates obtained from census findings would be useful. In this way, differences between the two special groups and the general population could be determined, enabling appropriate generalizations to be made.

Were subject and control issues adequately addressed in the literature, a major problem would still remain regarding measurement tools that have been utilized. Two basic procedures have been adopted in studies of the factors associated with death of a parent during childhood. One has been to match subjects who have lost a parent early with controls, and to assess the two groups on such factors as intelligence, academic achievement, personality, social skills, and emotional disturbance. The other technique has been to examine the family backgrounds of subjects who have already been identified as special in some way. Studies of geniuses and psychiatric patients have been conducted using this method of investigation. With both procedures, the use of inadequate or untested measurement tools to assess performance or identify characteristics such as emotional disturbance have led to doubts as to the meaning of the research. Basic to any scientific research is the use of instruments for evaluation which meet minimum standards of reliability and validity. Yet, as will be seen in the critical analysis to be conducted, many studies in this field have utilized informal means of assessment. Other studies have relied on psychiatric diagnoses as a way of differentiating among subjects. The questions that can be raised about the reliability and validity of the latter technique have been presented in the discussion of appropriate controls for emotionally disturbed populations. The determination of adequacy in measurement tools has been a difficult task in the behavioral sciences. Certainly untested instruments or those whose reliability or validity has been shown to be questionable should not be utilized, and on these counts a number of studies on the correlates of early parent death can be faulted.

A final general criticism must be directed at the fallacies in deduction made in many studies. Much of the research in this area is correlational, examining the variables that are associated with the experience of having a parent die during childhood. Unfortunately, researchers have gone beyond the data by asserting etiology based on findings of association, thereby ignoring possible intervening variables (Crook and Eliot 1980; Epstein et al. 1975; Gregory, 1958). Inferential statistics and longitudinal approaches to research that come closer to suggesting cause and effect relationships have not been used to any large extent. Thus, the numerous generalizations which have been made and are often logical from an intuitive perspective, cannot be accepted without question based on the empirical data offered as substantiation for them.

Procedures for Data Assessment

In the current critical analysis of the research on the child's adjustment and development following the death of a parent, an attempt will be made to incorporate the criticisms of the literature described above. A literature search of journals and books published in English within the disciplines of psychology, sociology, education, and medicine was conducted, utilizing relevant abstracts and research retrieval systems. Forty-five journals, twenty-four texts, and five papers presented at professional conferences were located. Table 2–1 contains a list of journals utilized. Over 200 sources are included in the review. Approximately one half are

Table 2–1
Journals Searched in the Literature Review

American Journal of Orthopsychiatry	Journal of Consulting and Clinical Psychology
American Journal of Psychiatry	Journal of Genetic Psychology
American Journal of Psychology	Journal of Genetics and Psychology
American Journal of Public Health	Journal of Mental Science
American Psychologist	Journal of Nervous and Mental Disease
Annual Review of Psychology	Journal of Projective Techniques
Archives of General Psychiatry	Journal of School Health
Archives of the Foundation of Thanatology	Journal of School Psychology
British Journal of Medical Psychology	Journal of the American Psychoanalytic Association
British Journal of Psychiatry	Marriage and Family Living
British Journal of Social Work	Mental Hygiene
Child Development	Omega
Child Psychiatry and Human Development	Pediatrics
Child Psychiatry Quarterly	Psychological Bulletin
Community Mental Health Journal	Psychological Medicine
Comprehensive Psychiatry	Psychological Reports
Contemporary Psychoanalysis	Psychology in the Schools
Death Education	Psychosomatic Medicine
Developmental Psychology	Social Casework
Family Coordinator	Social Forces
Journal of Child Psychology and Psychiatry	Social Psychiatry
Journal of Child Psychology, Psychiatry and Allied Disciplines	Young Children

empirical studies examining the relationship between death of a parent during childhood and an individual's subsequent adjustment and development. The other sources include literature reviews on some aspect of this topic, studies on outcomes of preventative mental health programs, research on the way in which the concept of death is acquired by children, and other scientific investigations relevant to the topics discussed. In addition, works which are not empirically oriented such as case studies, theoretical papers, and program descriptions will be included in the analysis. Primarily research conducted over the past twenty years was reviewed, as the more recent emphasis on methodological issues in the behavioral sciences was expected to yield more statistically sound and reliable studies. Selected earlier studies were also chosen due to their unique approach or content.

An attempt has been made to evaluate the methodological adequacy of the research. The two main bodies of empirical research, which deal with the development of the concept of death in children, and the correlates of experiencing death of a parent during childhood, are assessed. Criteria for evaluation are based on Maher's (1978) guidelines and on the critiques by the authors discussed above.

The research on development of the concept of death, which makes up a small proportion of the studies to be analyzed (fourteen of one hundred) and is somewhat peripheral to the major thrust of this review, has been rated on the following dimensions:

1. Were subjects matched or stratified on age, sex, and socioeconomic status (SES)?
2. How was development of the concept determined? Did the study use a cross sectional or longitudinal approach? If a cross sectional approach was used, were subjects in different age groups matched on sex and SES?
3. What measurement instruments were utilized? Were these tools documented as valid and reliable?
4. Were the data statistically analyzed? If so, were the techniques used appropriate to the data?

As these studies are less complex, and require analysis on fewer dimensions than do the parent death studies, and the criteria on which they are to be judged are all essential to their methodological integrity, the studies have been rated as either adequate or inadequate. Finer distinctions were necessary for the remaining studies.

The research on the correlates of experiencing death of a parent during childhood has been judged in accordance with the following questions:

1. Was the type of parental loss specified?

2. Was a comparison group specified?
3. Were subjects and controls matched on age, sex, and SES?
4. Was the subject group homogeneous on dimensions such as age, age at time of loss, SES, or if not, were these variables accounted for in the interpretation of results?
5. Were characteristics of the deceased parent specified?
6. What measurement instruments were utilized? Have these tools been documented as valid and reliable?
7. Were the data statistically analyzed? If so, were the techniques used appropriate to the data?
8. Were characteristics of family structure and living situations prior to and subsequent to the parent loss detailed?
9. Was informaton provided regarding the time at which subjects were assessed for research purposes relative to the time of the parent's death? Was this information considered in the analysis of the data?

Each study was then assigned to a category based on its relative level of methodological adequacy. Both the number and type of methodological strengths and weaknesses were considered in determining the character-istics of each level. Those procedures which are inconsistent with standard methods of scientific investigation were considered most important, while techniques or omissions which tended to cloud interpretation were judged as of relatively less importance. The model of evaluation is presented in table 2–2.

Studies were grouped by subject matter on independent, dependent, and process variables. Thus, many studies were analyzed and rated a number of times. Findings from these analyses were compared with con-clusions drawn in reviews of the literature by other researchers. Com-parisons were also made with published case studies and theoretical material on each subject.

Interaction effects of different independent and dependent variables, identified through a multidimensional analysis of individual, family and cultural issues, were evaluated. This approach was suggested by Shinn in her 1976 review of father absence and children's cognitive develop-ment. Shinn differentially related three general outcome measures: IQ, achievement-test scores, and school performance, to various independent variables involved in different spheres of influence on children's devel-opment: cause, duration, and onset of father's absence, child's age, sex, and SES, and mother's ability to compensate for the loss. In the current project, the extent to which these variables are accounted for in each study was determined and, in the final analysis of findings, only research in which certain minimal levels of methodological adequacy were achieved was considered.

Table 2–2
Model for Evaluating the Research

Level I[a]
Comparison group is present (or nonparametrics used).
Type of parent loss is specified.
Data is statistically analyzed, using appropriate techniques.
Sample is homogeneous on age, age at time of loss, SES, sex, or these variables are accounted for.
Comparison group is matched with sample on age, SES, sex.
Methods of assessment are documented as reliable and valid for use made of them.
Characteristics of deceased parent are detailed and accounted for in interpretation of results.
Time of assessment relative to when loss occurred is considered.
Characteristics of family structure and living situation before and after the loss are presented and either controlled for or analyzed in interpretation of study outcome.

Level II
Comparison group is present (or nonparametrics used).
Type of parent loss is specified.
Data is statistically analyzed, using appropriate techniques.
Sample is homogeneous on age, SES, sex or these variables are accounted for.
Comparison group is matched with sample on age, SES, sex.
Methods of assessment are documented as reliable, valid.

Level III
Comparison group is present (or nonparametrics used).
Type of parent loss is specified.
Data is statistically analyzed, using appropriate techniques, or could be determined from data provided.
Sample is homogeneous on age, SES, sex or these variables are accounted for.
Comparison group is matched with samples on two of the following: age, SES, sex.
Standard psychiatric diagnosis may be used as form of measurement. Less well-established diagnostic methods are not used.

Level IV
Comparison group is present (or nonparametrics used).
Type of parent loss is specified.
Data is statistically analyzed, using appropriate techniques, or could be determined from data provided.
Less well-established methods of measuring outcome or differentiating among groups, including nontraditional psychiatric diagnoses are used.
None of the other criteria listed above is necessarily included.

Level V
Comparison group lacking or type of loss is not specified.

[a]Level I indicates highest standards of methodological adequacy.

Studies were assessed also as to whether outcomes are in line with the authors' hypotheses. *Positive outcome* is the term used to indicate that the results supported the hypotheses while *negative outcome* refers to data in which no differences were found between groups. In most cases, it was not possible to determine whether outcome was in another direction from the hypothesis that was postulated. For example, in studies in which no evidence of disrupted development was present, the possibility that indications of adaptive mental health existed could not be determined.

Following the topic-by-topic assessment of methodological adequacy of research and the determination of outcomes and of interaction effects of different variables, the findings of these analyses were organized and integrated. Again, comparisons were made with literature reviews, case studies, and theoretical discussions. In this way, an attempt has been made to provide an overview of conclusions which can be drawn about differences which may, in fact, exist between those who have lost a parent during childhood and those who have not, and about the magnitude and sources of these possible differences.

3

Analysis of the Literature

The literature was analyzed in accordance with the procedures outlined in the previous chapter. This evaluation has been divided into three sections: (1) behaviors observed subsequent to the death of a parent; (2) relevant factors specific to the family situation and the circumstances surrounding the death, and (3) characteristics of the child that may influence the way in which she/he reacts to the death of a parent. Clearly, many studies will include information pertaining to all three of these categories; therefore, there are multiple analyses of a number of research reports. Following the evaluations of studies on each group of factors, an attempt has been made to integrate the analyses and to summarize the research results with regard to the relative levels of methodological adequacy of each study.

Behaviors Observed Subsequent to the Death of a Parent

In this section, what are generally regarded as dependent measures of outcome variables are discussed. Since much of the research is correlational and, in many studies, potential intervening variables are not considered, these behaviors should not be regarded as having been caused by the death of a parent. Related process or mediating variables are mentioned in this section and are analyzed in more detail later. The topics to be addressed include: (1) immediate reactions, (2) emotional disturbance, (3) personality, (4) sex role, sexual and related interpersonal functioning, (5) conscience development, juvenile delinquency and criminal behavior, and (6) cognitive, academic, scientific, and creative achievement.

Immediate Reactions of Children to the Death of a Parent

The literature focusing on the immediate reactions of children to the death of a parent has consisted primarily of theoretical papers attempting to explain the mechanisms underlying symptoms recorded in case studies, or comparing the intrapsychic similarities among responses to various forms of parent-child separations. There have been a few descriptive studies recording patterns of behavior displayed by groups of children observed a short time (presumably within a year) after a parent's death. None of this research is empirically oriented, and therefore could not be appropriately rated in accordance with the system described. (If our procedure were followed, no study would be rated above level V). However, this literature has been evaluated with respect to the methodological issues raised. This section is devoted to an analysis of the descriptive research, followed by a comparison of the results of this work and the positions of major theorists concerned with the subject.

The descriptive studies on children's immediate reactions to a parent's death can be faulted on many of the standards for methodological adequacy. This research has addressed loss through death as differentiated from other forms of loss. In only one study (Cain and Fast 1965) has the type of death been specified. Statistical analyses have been completely omitted, and few studies have included presentation of data regarding proportions of subjects showing different behaviors, or even sample sizes. Also lacking has been information on the ways in which data has been gathered. It must be assumed, therefore, that methods of demonstrated reliability and validity have not been utilized. In the absence of the use of such techniques, a full description of the ways in which data has been gathered (as type of interview, conditions under which observations were done and sources of information available in records) would have been useful in interpreting the material presented.

The deficit that most seriously hinders the ability of the reader of research on immediate reactions to a parent's death in drawing conclusions from the data has been the failure to adequately describe the samples employed. Such information as sex, age, and socioeconomic status of subjects is essential in determining the meaning and generalizability of research results. Such factors as temperament of the child, family structure, sex of the parent, and his/her relationship with the child, as well as changes in the living situation occurring immediately after the death have also been ignored, except in individual case studies.

Comparison groups have not been included in any of this research. It can be understood that the one-time comparison of recently bereaved and nonbereaved children would be of limited utility in providing an objective perspective on the subjects. Potentially more useful would be a longitudinal approach in which those with a critically ill parent are followed for some time before and after the death with a matched comparison group assessed over the same time period. Comparison groups would then be helpful in determining whether change has actually occurred and could be attributed to the bereavement.

Another way in which comparison groups might be utilized would be in exploring differences between children of different ages as to their immediate reactions to the death of a parent. It could be speculated that differences would be seen, especially in individuals of different levels of understanding of the concept of death, as age-related phenomena.

In light of this criticism of the research, these studies must be considered preliminary explorations, to be utilized in hypothesis generation for future investigations. Nevertheless, findings from these studies have been remarkably consistent with methodologically superior research on immediate reactions of adults to the deaths of significant others. Such symptoms as overt denial of the reality of the death, anxiety, depression, anger, guilt, somatic complaints, and disturbances in eating and sleeping have been found in studies of children (Cain and Fast 1965; Kirkpatrick et al. 1965, Nagaraja 1977; Silverman and Englander 1975), as well as in research on adults (for example, Lindeman, 1944; Rudestam 1977). Of interest is the fact that the researchers of children seemed to consider these behaviors psychopathological, while the authors of studies on adults appeared to view them as normal. This perspective may result from the views of theorists (summarized by Miller 1971) that children do not have the ability to mourn; therefore, all symptoms are regarded as abnormal. Other reactions observed in children have included reduced academic achievement, social withdrawal, rebellion, phobias, running away, accident proneness, and enuresis. Fear that the remaining parent would die and an excessive sense of responsibility for oneself and other family members were also seen in some children (Silverman and Englander 1975). A summary of these descriptive studies and the more theoretically oriented works is presented in table 3–1.

As was mentioned previously, most of the literature concerned with children's immediate reactions to a parent's death has been theoretical in nature, attempting to explain the dynamics underlying grief reactions. These discussions have been largely psychoanalytically oriented, drawing

Table 3–1
Summary of Literature on Immediate Reactions to a Parent's Death

Reference	Procedures	Results/Conclusions
Bowlby (1960)	Theory based on case-study material	Delineated three stages of mourning: 1. protest and denial 2. despair and disorganization 3. reorganization
Bowlby (1963)	Theory based on observations and case studies	Described process of mourning in childhood
Bowlby (1960)	Theory based on observations of institutionalized children	Likened reaction to separation to mourning process

Table 3–1 Continued

Reference	Procedures	Results/Conclusions
Cain and Fast (1965)	Observation and interpretation of behaviors of children with a parent who committed suicide; sample selected from coroner-report data	Indications of disturbed reactions: depression, reality distortion, relationship problems
Freud (reprinted in 1950)	Theoretical discussion based on case-study material	The "work of mourning" seen as extricating libidinal investment in the deceased
Freud (reprinted in 1957)	Theory based on case-study material	Related intrapsychic development to mourning process
Freud (reprinted in 1961)	Theory based on case-study material	Linked identification with the deceased as necessary condition for completion of mourning process
Furman (1964)	Theory based on child-therapy case studies	The childhood mourning process was explained
Furman (1973)	Theory based on child-therapy case studies	Described developmental prerequisites for mourning in childhood
Goldberg (1973)	Theory based on family-therapy case studies	Presented pattern of family tasks and reorganization after a death
Kirkpatrick et al. (1965)	Survey of school records	Disturbed behavior at home and school
Krupp (1972)	Review of theoretical and empirical material	Viewed extended family system and ritual as minimizing the disruptiveness of a death
Miller (1971)	Review of psychoanalytic literature	Found agreement among theorists that a pattern of reactions of children is universal and can be differentiated from that of adults
Moss and Moss (1973)	Theory presumably based on case material	Compared grief and separation experiences
Nagaraja (1977)	Case studies of four under-seven-year olds	Interpreted observations of denial, depression and neurotic behavior as pathological mourning
Rochlin (1967)	Review of theoretical and empirical material	Connected separation experiences with reactions to death
Silverman and Englander (1975)	Interviews with mothers of paternally bereaved children	Depression, denial, anxiety/withdrawal, fears, vegetative signs observed

heavily on the early works of Freud. The behaviors and attitudes examined have been consistent with those observed in larger group studies: denial, depression, guilt, anger, and somatic complaints.

The stages involved in the bereavement process have been delineated in similar terms by a number of authors. Bowlby (1960), for example, has described bereavement as beginning with (1) protest and denial, progressing to (2) despair and personal disorganization, and, finally, 3) reorganization, which involves the transfer of affective attachment to new relationships. Moss and Moss (1973) and Freud (1950, 1957, 1961) have organized their observations of the bereavement process in like fashion. Moss and Moss (1973) have observed that this process is quite similar to that experienced by individuals who must come to terms with their own imminent death. Kubler-Ross, in her classic study of 1969, presented the stages of dying as (1) denial, (2) rage and anger, (3) bargaining, (4) depression, (5) acceptance. Only the resolution of the affective experiences of the dying and the bereaved, acceptance versus investment in new relationships differs, in accordance with the contrasting situations of the two groups.

All later psychoanalytic interpretations of the work of mourning appear to have been based on Freud's "Mourning and Melancholia" (reprinted in 1950). In it, he proposes that the mourner attempts to deny the death of a loved one as long as possible. When reality necessitates acceptance, there is some anxiety regarding the individual's own mortality, and this anxiety facilitates adjustment to the loss. Freud termed this gradual withdrawal of affective energy "decathexes of the internal representation of the lost love object."

Most writers, including Freud, have hypothesized that the quality of the mourning experience is different for the child and the adult. Freud, in "On Narcissism" (reprinted in 1957), questioned the child's ability to comprehend death and, therefore, to mourn in an appropriate and useful manner. He stated that such "cardinal" characteristics of children as the belief in the omnipotence of wishes, the sense of helplessness and dread of abandonment, the preoccupation with causality, and egocentrism prevent children from completing the work of mourning, causing them instead to turn to magical thinking: death can be defied. Similar processes have been observed in empirical studies based on the work of Piaget. This material will be discussed in the section on the development of the concept of death.

Miller, in her 1971 review of psychoanalytic works of such authors as Abraham, Deutsh, Freud, Mahler, and Neubaur, concluded that there was a concensus that children do not experience true mourning, which she defined as "the gradual and painful emotional detachment from the inner representation of the person who has died." Instead, children, specifically those who have lost a parent through death, respond with such manifestations of denial as unconscious or conscious denial of the reality of the parent's death, increased identification with and idealization of the parent who has died, avoidance of the expression of affective responses to the death, fantasies about an on-going relationship, and decreased self-esteem.

There is not total agreement about the inability to mourn, however. Both Furman (1964, 1973) and Bowlby (1960, 1963) have posited that children can and do go through the process. According to Furman, the presence of the following skills and characteristics are necessary before mourning can take place: (1) understanding of the concept of death, (2) object constancy, (3) a "healthy availability of feeling not being excessively defended against," (4) a flexible personality structure, (5) knowledge that one's physical and emotional-survival needs will be met, and (6) acceptance of expressions of feeling by others in the environment. Furman has ventured that these conditions might be met in a four-year old, a contention with which researchers on the development of the concept of death would disagree, as will be seen.

Furman's conceptualization suggests that the utilization of a developmental perspective might be more appropriate than the artificial differentiation between the responses to death of adults and children. The development of the concept of death, one of Furman's prerequisites to the capacity for mourning, may begin in infancy with the gradual process of coming to understand and accept separations. Bowlby (1968) and Moss and Moss (1973) have conceived of separation as a death-like experience, involving similar physical, environmental, emotional, and social characteristics. The infant's response to separations, anger, protest, and despair, are not unlike the responses of the child and the adult to death. Investigation of the difficulty and degree to which early-separation issues were resolved in children with varying responses to a parent's death might be one way of exploring the relationship between reactions to death and separation. Longitudinal research on other aspects of Furman's model would be helpful in determining the course of development of the capacity for mourning.

Some attention has been given to factors outside of the individual by theorists seeking to explain immediate responses to death. Goldberg (1973), for example, has viewed death as a family crisis, an infrequent and final event for which new problem-solving skills must be developed. The tasks of the bereaved family, according to Goldberg, include discontinuation of the use of the memory of the deceased as a functional force in family activities, reassignment of roles within the family, and assumption of new roles outside of the family. Both positive and negative options, such as role reorganization, increased family cohesiveness, establishment of new relationships, and scapegoating as a way of displacing anger about the death, may be available to the family, depending on their history and currently available resources.

Krupp (1972) has suggested that the presence of the extended family is important in decreasing the trauma of death because its continued collective identity, the shared sense of responsibility, and the provision of alternative sources of affection lessen the pain of separation. He has maintained that the demise of the extended family has made accepting death more difficult. He has also pointed out the importance of ritual in facilitating appropriate mourning by "channeling and legitimizing the normal expression of grief, rallying friends, and establishing new roles."

At this point in the accumulation of literature on children's immediate reactions to the death of a parent, there exist only hypotheses about what typically occurs in such a situation. It would seem that the descriptive research suggests that children do go through a process of mourning, and that this process is quite similar to that experienced by adults. It would be expected that differences with respect to age would be seen, in light of research showing that children do not fully understand the concept of death until middle childhood (for example, Kane 1979), as will be discussed later in this book. Cross-sectional research on children of different ages would clarify this notion.

It is clear that both research and theory of children's immediate reactions to the death of a parent are in need of further refinement. It appears that there has been more emphasis on theory, so that there are elaborate explanations of processes and causes for reactions that may occur seldom, if at all. Further empirical research, ideally from a developmental perspective, that would examine the reactions of individuals within personal, family, and social context, would help to balance the literature in this area. Suggestions for the nature of this research can come from previously conducted descriptive studies that would benefit from validation through use of more methodologically rigorous procedures, and from hypotheses of theorists. Revision of theoretical notions may become more appropriate following the accumulation of empirical data.

Emotional Disturbance

Among the studies, theoretical works, and literature reviews on behaviors observed subsequent to a parent's death, the largest number (sixty-one) have dealt with some form of emotional disturbance manifested either in childhood or when the bereaved child reaches adulthood. There can be speculation on two possible reasons for this emphasis in the literature. One explanation might be that those who have lost a parent through death during childhood are overrepresented in emotionally disturbed populations. Ideas for such studies may have come from informal observations of bereaved children in schools or clinical situations. The other possibility is that the expectation that early death of a parent is associated with emotional disturbance has influenced the researchers' choice of topics. Support for the latter line of reasoning comes from the typical way in which this research has been conducted. Rather than following randomly selected bereaved and nonbereaved subjects and assessing their development, researchers have examined the family backgrounds of those already identified as emotionally disturbed.

Depression and suicidal behavior have been the most frequently investigated topics within the area of emotional disturbance. Nearly one-half of the studies on emotional disorders have dealt with depression and suicidal behavior. Again, expectations of researchers may have played a part in the emphasis on these forms of psychopathology. It is interesting, for example, that there are few studies examining the relationship between parental death and anxiety disorders. In clinical situations, it is recognized that many of the symptoms of anxiety and depression (sleeping and eating disturbances, somatic complaints, social withdrawal) are often similarly manifested. Traditional expectations have been for depression to follow a death, although a case could be made for the same to be true of anxiety. Reactions to the death of a parent might be expected to include uncertainty about the health or survival of the parent or the child himself/herself, for example.

The comments above are meant to indicate two ways in which expectations of researchers may influence the literature in this field. Expectations can affect the interpretations of outcomes; for example, an anxious patient may be seen as one who is depressed. In addition, assumptions may work to limit the range of topics explored; for example, exploration of the backgrounds of patients diagnosed as depressed, but not of those diagnosed as anxious. There may, in fact, be major gaps in the research investigating the relationship between parent death during childhood and emotional disturbance. Topics related to emotional disturbance, which have been researched relative to their relationship to parental death, have included depression and suicidal behavior, schizophrenia, paranoid psychosis, and general maladjustment, as determined by referral or admission to a mental-health facility, observations, or ratings on a scale of psychological adjustment. Studies on difficulties usually not considered or treated as emotional disturbance, such as delinquency and marital maladjustment will be discussed in later sections. The forms of emotional disturbance to be considered here are diverse in symptomatology but far from inclusive in terms of the range of possible psychological disorders. Again the literature may be reflecting the actual pattern of disorders found in bereaved individuals rather than the lack of research on other forms of disturbance. Studies yielding negative results on non-controversial subjects are infrequently published. There may very well be numerous pieces of research showing that parental bereavement during childhood is not associated with the development of phobias or obsessive-compulsive disorders.

The remainder of this chapter is devoted to presentation and discussion of the results of the systematic evaluation of the research on death of a parent during childhood and the subsequent emotional disturbance in bereaved children. The observations of other authors are incorporated, as are implications for future work in the area.

Forty-seven empirical studies dealing with psychopathology were reviewed and rated in accordance with the system of evaluation of research presented in chapter 2. Detailed results of this analysis are presented in table 3–2. A miscalculation was found by the author of one of the studies (Roy 1978), and a revised study was published the next year (Roy 1979). The original study has therefore been excluded from further interpretations of the data.

General results of the analysis along with a breakdown of ratings by outcome are shown in table 3–3. As can be seen, only one study, Shepherd and Barraclough (1976), could be included in category I. This study was methodologically adequate and descriptively complete on all of the criteria examined. A comparison group was utilized, and subjects and controls were matched for age, sex, marital status, and geographical area. Subjects and controls were randomly selected from families of one hundred consecutively reported suicides and two physician's medical practices. The study was restricted to children of suicide victims, a fine distinction within the general condition of parent loss seldom made in the literature. Observations were made over a five-to-seven-year period following the suicide, and consideration was given to the child's age at the time of the death in interpretations of the results. Measurement took the form of structured interviews with the remaining parent which were subsequently coded. Reliability was assessed by nine interviews involving two interviewers with one presenting the questions and both independently coding the responses. A reliability level of .94 was obtained. Referral rates for mental-health services were also considered.

Characteristics of the deceased parent and prior and subsequent family structure and living situation were presented in detail and related differentially to the results. The deceased parent's sex, mental health, marital relationship and marital status, the presence of a criminal record, and the circumstances surrounding any communication on the suicide were considered. Information about and determination of the significance of family size, birth order, changes in family makeup, incuding siblings leaving the home and the addition of a step-parent, changes in residence and

Table 3–2
Methodological Data and Adequacy Ratings on Empirical Studies on Emotional Disturbance and Parent Death in Childhood

Reference	Subject	Comparison Group Present	Group Matching (sex, age, SES)	Specify Type Loss	Statistical Sign Test
Abrahams and Whitlock (1969)	1. Depression 2. Psychiatric hospitalization	X	Inpatient depressives compared with general hospital outpatients. Matched on age, SES, sex, marital status.	X	X
Adam (1973)	Suicidal ideation and behavior	X	University clinic clients. Three groups: 1. parent death 2. parents divorced 3. intact family. Age, SES matching	X	X
Archibald et al. (1962)	Emotional disturbance: Depression, Psychosis, Hypochondriosis, Hysteria, Sex-role disturbance	X	Compared VA clinic patients with normative estimates of brereavement by Life Insurance Company. Demographic differences accounted for.	X	X
Barry and Lindemann (1960)	General maladaptation	X	Psychiatric inpatients compared with normative estimates of bereavement from life insurance tables. Demographic matching.	X	X
Beck, Sethi, Tuthill (1963)	Depression	X	Inpatients at psychiatric hospital compared on rating scale. Demographic data accounted for.	X	X
Bendiksen and Fulton (1975)	General maladaption	X	General bereaved population followed longitudinally. Demographically matched.	X	X
Birtchnell (1966)	Depression	X	Depressed and nondepressed state-hospital inpatients matched for age initially, not after second division.	X	X
Birtchnell (1970a)	Depression; suicidal behavior	X	Suicidal psychiatric inpatients compared with nonsuicidal inpatients. Matched age, sex accounted for.	X	X

Outcome Measure/Outcome	Could Study Be Repli-cated?[a]	Time of Assessment Loss	Characteristics of Deceased Parent	Family Structure	Rating
Diagnosis of different levels of depression. Found ND between depressives and others.	X	Not specified	NI	NI	III
Clinical interviews scored for presence/absence of suicidal ideation. Higher ideation in Groups #1 and 2.	X	Assessment at 17–27; Loss prior to 16	NI	NI	II
MMPI, psychiatric diagnosis. Overrepresentation of parentally bereaved in clinic population. Symptoms: neurotic, psychotic, psychophysiologic	X	Specifies age at admission	Sex specified	NI	II
Psychiatric diagnosis, Clinical interview. Parent death x Parent sex x child sex x age at loss interactions. Overrepresentation of bereaved patients.	X	Differentiated by time of loss	Sex specified	NI	III
Psychiatric diagnosis; standardized depression self-rating scale. More parentally bereaved among the depressed as identified by psychiatric diagnosis only.	X	Differentiated by time of loss	NI	NI	III
Behavioral observations and ratings. Some differences (depression) seen in middle age, fewer than in childhood.	X	Both accounted for	Sex specified	NI	II
Psychiatric diagnosis ND between groups. Differences between severely and moderately depressed found. More mother death in severely depressed.	X	Differentiated by age at loss	sex	NI	III
Overt behavioral observations. Overrepresentation of bereaved and illegitimate among suicidal patients.	X	Age at loss specified	NI	NI	II

Table 3–2 Continued

Reference	Subject	Comparison Group Present	Group Matching (sex, age, SES)	Specify Type Loss	Statistical Sign Test
Birtchnell (1970b)	General psychiatric disturbance	X	Psychiatric inpatients compared with outpatients. Age, sex matching, SES accounted for.	X	X
Birtchnell (1972)	Depression	X	Psychiatric inpatients compared with outpatient. Age matching, sex, SES accounted for.	X	X
Birtchnell (1975)	Characteristics of psychiatric inpatients	X	Psychiatric inpatients of various psychiatric diagnoses compared. Age, sex matching.	X	X
Brill and Liston (1966)	Psychiatric hospitalization	X	Psychiatric inpatients compared, age and sex matched	X	X
Brown (1961)	Depression	X	Psychiatric inpatients compared with insurance-table norms. Sex matched.	X	X
Brown, Harris, and Copeland (1977)	Depression	X	Depressed and non-depressed inpatients, neurotic nonpatients, and normals compared. All women, no SES matching.	X	X
Cain and Fast (1965)	Behavior of clinic patients	X	Bereaved versus non-bereaved child: clinic clients compared. Age and sex matched.	X	Percentages only (Figured for this analysis)
Caplan and Douglas (1969)	Depression	X	Depressed versus non-depressed psychiatric inpatient. No matching.	X	X
Crook and Raskin (1975)	Depression; suicide attempts	X	Depressed inpatients with suicidal attempts versus nonsuicidal depressed versus normals. Matched on sex and age.	X	X
Dennehy (1966)	Depression	X	Depressed psychiatric inpatients compared with 1921 census figures.	X	X

Outcome Measure/Outcome	Could Study Be Replicated?[a]	Time of Assessment Loss	Charac- teristics of Deceased Parent	Family Structure	Rating
Psychiatric hospital admission. Some differences (age x age at loss) found.	X	Both specified	Sex specified	NI	II
Psychiatric diagnosis. Higher percentage depressed in-patients were parentally be-reaved.	X	Both specified	Sex specified	NI	III
MMPI and case histories. Sex x parent sex, difference on dependency score.	X	Age at death	Sex specified	NI	II
Inpatient admission. Only father loss for reasons other than death significant.	X	NI	Sex specified	NI	II
Psychiatric diagnosis higher percentage parental death in depressed.	X	NI	NI	NI	III
Psychiatric diagnosis. Age at loss x sex of patient, differ-ences in depressed found.	X	Both specified	Sex specified	NI	III
Intake data, psychiatric diagnosis. ND in parental bereavement except in psy-chosis (more bereaved).	X	Both specified as well as time in between	Sex specified	NI	II
Psychiatric diagnosis. Sig-nificant differences only for those institutionalized early.	X	Both specified	NI	NI	IV
Psychiatric diagnoses. Case history of attempts. More parent loss among suicidal except for loss through death.	X	Age at loss	NI	NI	III
Psychiatric diagnosis. Sex x sex of parent x age at loss differences; higher bereave-ment rates in depressives.	X	Age at loss	Sex specified	NI	III

Table 3-2 Continued

Reference	Subject	Comparison Group Present	Group Matching (sex, age, SES)	Specify Type Loss	Statistical Sign Test
Dietrich (1979)	Psychopathic personality; death fear	X	College students from intact, parent-absent families. Matched on demographics.	X	X
Earle and Earle (1959)	Depression	X	Psychiatric inpatients from intact and mother-absent families. Age and sex matched.	X	X
Felner, Stolberg, and Cowen (1975)	Childhood maladjustment	X	Normal versus school-referred maladapted children matched on age and sex, SES expected equivalent	X	X
Forrest, Fraser and Priest et al. (1965)	Depression	X	Psychiatric versus general-hospital patients. Age and sex differences accounted for.	X	X
Gay and Tonge (1967)	Depression	X	Inpatients of various psychiatric diagnoses. No matching.	X	X
Granville-Grossman (1966)	Schizophrenia	X	Siblings compared.	X	X
Greer (1964)	Suicide attempt	X	Suicidal versus nonsuicidal inpatients. Matched on age, SES, sex.	X	X
Greer (1966)	Suicide attempt	X	Suicidal versus nonsuicidal inpatients. Matched on age, SES, sex.	X	X
Gregory (1966)	General emotional disturbance	X	Psychiatric inpatients of various diagnoses matched on age and sex.	X	X
Hilgard and Newman (1963)	Schizophrenia	X	Three groups: schizophrenic inpatients, alcoholic inpatients, and SES-sex-age matched controls.	X	X

Outcome Measure/Outcome	Could Study Be Repli- cated?[a]	Time of Assessment Loss	Charac- teristics of Deceased Parent	Family Structure	Rating
MMPI, TAT, Rosenzweig, Picture Frustration Test, Lester and Templer Death Fear Scale. Parent death *x* child's sex *x* age at loss dif- ferences on Pd, Mf, Pt, Sc MMPI scales.	X	Age at loss	NI	NI	II
Psychiatric diagnosis. Depression more common in maternally deprived.	X	Age at loss	Sex specified	NI	III
AML checklist, teacher-re- ferral form. Bereaved group more anxious, depressed, withdrawn.	X	Both specified	NI	NI	II
Psychiatric diagnosis. Early parent death higher among the depressed.	X	Age at loss	Sex specified	NI	III
Psychiatric diagnosis, case record. Reactive depression associated with early death of opposite sex, depression, other neuroses associated with death of same-sex parent.	Not easily	Age at loss	Sex specified	NI	IV
Psychiatric diagnosis. ND.	X	Age at loss	NI	NI	III
Suicide attempt. More suicidal had experienced parent loss in general, ND as to cause of loss.	X	Both specified	NI	NI	II
Suicide attempt. More suicidal had lost both par- ents, ND as to cause of loss.	Not with equi-dis- tribution as to type loss	Both specified	NI	NI	II
Psychiatric diagnoses. ND among psychiatric diag- noses.	X	NI	NI	NI	III
Psychiatric diagnosis. Sig- nificant differences for schizophrenics.	X	Age at admission	Sex specified	NI	III

Table 3-2 Continued

Reference	Subject	Compari-son Group Present	Group Matching (sex, age, SES)	Specify Type Loss	Statistical Sign Test
Hill (1969)	Depression, suicide	X	Two groups of depressed, inpatients, one suicidal, age controlled.	X	X
Hill and Price (1967)	Depression	X	Endogenous and reactive depressed inpatients compared. Controlled for age.	X	X
Hopkinson and Reed (1966)	Depression	X	Groups of psychiatric inpatients of various diagnoses, age, SES, no controls.	X	X
Huttunen and Niska-nen (1978)	Schizophrenia	X	Subjects who lost father prenatally compared with Ss who lost a father during first year. SES and age matched.	X	X
Jacobson, Fasman, and DiMascio (1975)	Depression	X	Normal controls versus depressed inpatients versus depressed outpatients. Sex and age matched.	X	X
Kirkpatrick et al. (1965)	School adjustment	No		X	No
Lester and Beck (1976)	Suicide attempt	No		X	X
Martindale (1972)	General emotional disturbance	No		Yes—but death and others indiscriminately grouped	No Percentages
Munro (1966)	Depression	X	Depressed inpatients and age-and-sex-matched general-hospital controls compared.	X	X
Munro and Griffiths (1968)	Depression	X	Psychiatric inpatients, outpatients, and general-hospital patients. Age, geographic location matched.	X	X

Outcome Measure/Outcome	Could Study Be Replicated?[a]	Time of Assessment Loss	Characteristics of Deceased Parent	Family Structure	Rating
Suicide attempt, psychiatric diagnosis. Suicide attempts more common in depressed women who lost fathers.	X	Age at loss	Sex specified	NI	III
Psychiatric diagnoses of endogenous versus reactive depression. Age at loss x sex differences found.	Diagnosis would be difficult to replicate	Age at loss	Sex specified	NI	IV
Psychiatric diagnoses. ND.	X	Age at loss	Type death, psychiatric diagnosis	NI	IV
Psychiatric diagnosis. Higher percentage schizophrenics lost father prenatally.	X	Both specified	Sex specified	NI	III
Psychiatric diagnosis. ND.	X	NI	NI	NI	III
School records. Changes in level of adjustment following parent death.	Not easily	Age at loss	Sex specified	NI	V
Suicide attempt. A recent death and death of both parents before associated with a suicide attempt.	X	Age at loss	NI	NI	V
Listing in Oxford Anthology of Verse, life histories. Relationship between psychopathology and father loss unclear.	X	NI	Sex specified	NI	V
Psychiatric diagnosis severe versus moderate depression. ND between groups on different types of loss.	Not easily	NI	Quality of relationship with deceased parent, parent's sex	NI	IV
Psychiatric diagnosis. Inpatient depressives showed excess of maternal bereavement.	X	NI	Sex specified	NI	III

Table 3–2 Continued

Reference	Subject	Compari-son Group Present	Group Matching (sex, age, SES)	Specify Type Loss	Statistical Sign Test
Pitts et al. (1965)	General emo-tional disturb-ance	X	Affectively disordered in-patients matched on age, sex, SES and marital sta-tus with medical patients.	X	X
Roy (1978) (Not counted in future tabulations)	Depression	X	Depressed versus gyn pa-tients X matched on age, SES, m.d.	X	X
Roy (1979)	Depression	X	Same as above.	X	X
Seligman and Glesser (1974)	Clinic referral	X	Clinic referral compared X with general school population and other medical referrals. No matching.	X	No
Sethi (1964)	Depression	X	Psychiatric inpatients compared with each other. No matching.	X	X
Shepherd and Barra-clough (1976)	Psychological maladjustment	X	Families of suicide vic-tims matched with fami-lies randomly selected from general practice of MDs. Matched for age, sex, m.s., and geo-graphic area.	X	X
Trunnell (1968)	Psychological maladjustment	X	Father present, absent. No clinic subjects, matched on age, SES.	X	X
Tuckman and Regan (1966)	Clinic referral	X	Age matching of children in homes with separation divorce and parent death.	X	X
Walton (1958)	Suicide attempt	X	Suicidal versus nonsuici-dal. No depressed clinic clients. No matching.	No	X
Wilson, All-top, and Buffaloe (1967)	Variations in depressive profile	X	Consecutively admitted depressed inpatients who were from intact or par-ent death families.	X	X

NI = no information provided

[a]2—In studies where traditional psychiatric diagnoses were utilized, this item is checked affirm-atively although reliability and validity is questionable.

Outcome Measure/Outcome	Could Study Be Repli- cated?[a]	Time of Assessment Loss	Charac- teristics of Deceased Parent	Family Structure	Rating
Psychiatric diagnosis. ND on family background.	X	NI	Sex specified	NI	III
Psychiatric diagnosis. More depressed had had a parent die; figures in error.	X (and was)	NI	NI	NI	V
Psychiatric diagnosis. Cor- rected parental bereavement above, ND. Roy (1978)	X	NI	NI	NI	III
Clinic referral. Higher per- cent (more than 2x) of par- ent death in clinic group.	X	NI	Sex specified	NI	IV
Depression inventory. ND among depressives.	Not with regard to sample	NI	NI	NI	IV
Long term observations strangers, inteviews with high reliability. Prior and subsequent family conditions x loss differences.	X	Followed 5–7 years after suicide	Detailed	Prior, subse- quent family situation detailed	I
Psychiatric-diagnosis case record. Environmental fac- tors x parent characteristics x individual characteristics in- tragroup differences.	X	Age at loss	Detailed	Prior, subse- quent family situation detailed	III
Clinic referral. More clinic- referral problems in homes with separation and divorce.	X	NI	Sex specified	Specula- tion con- cerning	II
Reports of attempts or threats of suicide. Psychiat- ric diagnosis. More suicidals had been parentally de- prived.	No	NI	NI	NI	IV
Psychiatric diagnosis. MMPI. Parentally bereaved had higher scores on the psychotic tetrad.	X	NI	Sex specified	NI	III

Table 3–3
Ratings of Studies of Emotional Disturbance, by Outcome

Rating	Total Number	Positive Outcome	Negative Outcome[a]
I	1	1	0
II	13	10	3
III	22	15	7
IV	8	4	4
V	3	2	1
Totals	47	32	15

[a]Under this category are included studies in which differences are not associated with parent death, or when this relationship is unclear, even when methodological errors overlooked.

socioeconomic status, as well as changes in parent-child relationships were included. Two omissions were data concerning the child's relationship with the deceased parent and information about the child's previous level of functioning. Even with this flaw, Shepherd and Barraclough's study significantly surpassed all others reviewed. Results of this investigation will be described in the section on general maladjustment. It should be noted at this point that it was shown that children of a parent who committed suicide differed from those who had not lost a parent.

Thirteen of the forty-seven studies met the criteria for a level-II rating. These studies were flawed primarily as a result of the failure to include descriptions of, and therefore to account for, characteristics of the family and the child's age at the time of the parent's death. Most included the sex of the deceased parent, which was not necessary for a rating at this level. The studies were all concerned with either general maladjustment indications (primarily admisson to a mental-health facility) and suicidal behavior. None of the research on psychosis and general depression (without suicidal behavior considered) was rated above level III. Seventy-seven percent of the level-II studies yielded positive outcomes. Outcomes were considered negative if differences were not associated specifically with parent death, or when this relationship remained unclear even when methodological errors were overlooked.

The modal rating among these studies was level III. Twenty-two of the studies, including research on all areas of emotional disturbance, met the criteria for this level. In general, the studies looked much like those of level II, except for the methods used for assessing difference among groups. Studies in this category frequently used standard psychiatric diagnoses as a means of differentiating among subjects and controls or in evaluating outcome. The studies varied with regard to inclusion of information on the subject's age at the time of the loss and the time of assessment, characteristics of the deceased parent, and on family structure and living situation. Fifteen of the twenty-two studies showed differences between those who were parentally bereaved during childhood and those in comparison groups.

Level IV included eight studies, four of which yielded positive results. These studies were distinguished from those at level III because the latter contain inadequacies in the makeup of comparison groups or in measurement instruments. Matching on factors such as age, sex, and socioeconomic status was not documented in some of the studies. In others, differences between groups were assessed by methods that were not well described and therefore could not be replicated. Unorthodox psychiatric diagnoses were among these techniques. Studies on suicidal behavior, depression, and general maladjustment were included in this categorization.

The three level-V studies (apart from Roy 1978) were concerned with general maladjustment, depression, and suicidal behavior, and two showed differences between those who had lost a parent through death and those who had not. All three were lacking control groups, and two were not analyzed statistically. These studies did specify the type of loss the child experienced but it should be noted that most of those that did not differentiate among subjects on this basis were eliminated as the literature search for this project was being conducted.

Even with the methodological flaws overlooked, the results of the studies remain equivocal. Ten of the studies associate parental bereavement with the development of depression in adulthood, but eight of the studies could show no such association. These results differ from those of Crook and Eliot (1980). They concur that the relationship between depression and childhood bereavement has not been established, but assert that studies supporting this association have been methodologically flawed, while those showing no such relationship have been well controlled. These contrasting conclusions can be accounted for by differences in the specific studies reviewed and variation in the criteria on which the research was evaluated. Crook and Eliot accepted psychiatric diagnosis as a valid measurement tool, for example.

Sixteen studies have been categorized under the heading of general maladjustment including one at level I and seven at level II. This category is less homogeneous than those described above as it is comprised of studies associating parent death with children's referral to programs for maladjustment in school, admission to clinics and psychiatric hospitals, and scores indicating problems in mental health on standardized rating scales. The results of these relatively sound studies (six positive outcomes, two negative) must therefore be examined individually. There would otherwise have been many more studies in this category.

In general, the higher-level studies yielded a higher proportion of positive results than did the lower-level studies. When levels I through IV are considered (level V was excluded since the total number of studies that would be so rated is artificially low due to prescreening of studies that did not differentiate among causes of loss), positive-to-negative study ratios are 11:3 for the higher level studies and for lower level studies. Thus 73 percent of the levels I and II studies had positive outcomes compared to 57 percent of the levels-III and -IV studies.

Ratings of studies on emotional disturbance by specific disorder and outcome are presented in table 3–4. As can be seen, four of the eight studies on suicidal behavior are rated at level II, with two having positive outcomes and two yielding negative outcomes. The remaining, less methodologically adequate, studies include four with positive results and one with negative results.

The four level-II studies linking suicidal behavior with loss of a parent during childhood include those by Adam (1973), Birtchnell (1970a), and Greer (1964, 1966). Three of the four studies used as outcome measure actual suicide attempts or completed suicides while Adam made use of structured clinical interviews scored for the presence or absence of suicidal ideation. In two of the studies there was a higher frequency of those who had experienced the loss of a parent in general, but those experiencing a parent's death did not differ from those who had lost a parent for other reasons. Thus parent death, as well as other forms of parent loss, was associated with subsequent suicidal behavior or ideation. The studies therefore showed a higher incidence of suicidal behavior among adult psychiatric inpatients who had experienced loss of a parent over those from intact families.

Of the eighteen studies on depression that do not consider the presence or absence of suicidal behavior, twelve were categorized as level III and six as level IV. These investigations were, for the most part, concerned with examining the family backgrounds of psychiatric patients diagnosed as depressed. It was the use of psychiatric diagnoses as the primary means of assessment or differentiation that resulted in relatively low ratings for the research. As was discussed previously, psychiatric diagnoses have been shown to have poor reliability in differentiating among specific categories of disorders. In the case of associations between aspects of an individual's background and psychiatric diagnosis, the problem would be confounded, as psychiatric diagnoses are usually based, at least in part, on case histories.

The procedures used in the one level I study, Shepherd and Barraclough (1976) were described above, and the results were mentioned in the general methodology section (chapter 2). Children were assessed on whether treatment was being received for psychological problems, reg-

Table 3-4
Ratings of Studies on Emotional Disturbance, by Disorder and Outcome

Rating Outcome	I			II			III			IV			V			Totals by disorder		
	+	−	Total	+	−	Total	+	−	Total	+	−	Total	+	−	Total	+	−	Total
Suicidal Behavior	0	0	0	2	2	4	2	1	3	1	0	1	1	0	1	6	3	9
Depression (in studies where suicidal behavior is not considered)	0	0	0	0	0	0	8	3	11	2	4	6	0	0	0	10	7	17
General maladjustment, admission to mental health facility	1	0	1	7	1	8	2	2	4	1	0	1	1	1	2	12	4	16
Psychosis	0	0	0	1	0	1	3	1	4	0	0	0	0	0	0	4	1	5
Totals, by rating	1	0	1	10	3	12	15	7	22	4	4	8	2	1	3	32	15	47

ularity of school attendance and school-related difficulty, quality of relationship with the surviving parent and other family members, and other information obtained from structured interviews with the parent. Of the thirty-one children on whom there were sufficient data (the five on whom data were insufficient were described but not rated), fifteen children were assessed as functioning adequately and sixteen as not. Differences between children of different adjustment levels were not found on age, sex, socioeconomic status, sex of the parent lost, or characteristics of the suicide. Only children were judged to be functioning more adequately. Very significant were differences in family life before the suicide. Those whose parents had been separated, had criminal records or mental health problems, adjusted less well after the parent's death. Also important was stability of life after the suicide. Those who attended more than two schools (which is presumed to represent either changes in residence, or economic status, or both) were shown to have more problems. This study thus indicates the importance of consideration of multiple factors related to the family situation before and after a parent's death in any interpretation of subsequent functioning of a child.

The level-II studies differed from the level I study in neglecting to consider family characteristics. Two of the studies (Brill and Liston 1966, and Birtchnell 1970b) looked at the representation of the parentally bereaved among psychiatric inpatients with differing results. Brill and Liston found that only individuals who had lost a father for reasons other than death were overrepresented among inpatients. In contrast, Birtchnell found recent (in the previous five years) father death in patients in their early twenties to have occurred at a rate greater than would have been expected. Neither study found that death of a mother or of either parent was more frequent among subjects than among controls.

Level-II research utilizing adjustment scales was concerned with identification of characteristics or tendencies, for the most part, among clinic or psychiatric hospital patients, rather than global patterns of behavior. They showed that among the parentally bereaved were individuals who were prone towards dependency, withdrawal, anxiety, and acting out. Studies concerned with these characteristics will be examined again in the section on personality, which reviews studies on nonpsychiatric-patient subjects in order to determine whether any consistent pattern emerges.

Four of the five studies dealing with psychosis were rated at level III. All of the research on this general disorder utilized psychiatric diagnoses for differentiating between groups. One of the studies, Cain and Fast (1965) utilized broad categorizations, distinguishing psychoses from other disorders, which produced a higher degree of reliability (Quay 1979). Thus, this study, which met all of the other criteria for level II, could be rated higher than the other studies, which differentiated among psychotic disorders. Cain and Fast found that children who had had a parent who committed suicide were overrepresented among those diagnosed as psychotic in a clinic population. Investigation into the prior mental health of these children would aid in determining whether the parents' suicides contributed to the children's maladjustment or whether the children's problems were among the stresses that led vulnerable parents to suicide. The level-III studies found a higher proportion of schizophrenics had lost a mother (Hilgard and Newman 1963) or a father (Huttunen and Niskanen 1978) and that psychiatrically diagnosed depressives who were parentally bereaved had higher scores on the psychotic indicators of the MMPI (Wilson, Alltop, and Buffaloe 1967). Granville-Grossman (1966) looked at schizophrenics and their nonschizophrenic siblings and found no relationship between the child's age at the death of the parent and the development of schizophrenia.

There are, then, positive outcomes for just over half of the studies on emotional disturbance that meet minimal standards for methodological adequacy (levels I and II). Remaining, however, are a number of satis factory studies with negative results, as well as the flawed research that makes up the largest portion of work in this area. Herzog and Sudia (1973) have taken the position that such evidence must be considered ambiguous because of both the conflicting data and the poor quality of the research. Brown (1966) concludes that, despite the problems, there has been shown to be some association between various forms of emotional disturbance and parental bereavement in childhood. This interpretation seems reasonable in light of the positive outcomes of some of the better studies. Invariably these have shown that there are complex relationships among various environmental and child-specific factors and the major independent and dependent variables, parental bereavement and manifestations of emotional disturbance. A unidimensional cause-and-effect association is unlikely to be uncovered; nor would such a finding be expected on a logical basis. Thus, in order to determine further the relationship between death of a parent during childhood and subsequent emotional disorders, research must consider multiple variables in a systematic manner.

Personality

Research on personality variables, as differentiated from manifestations of emotional disturbance requiring professional treatment, has made up a relatively small proportion of the literature on the correlates of parental bereavement during childhood. The aspects of functioning to be examined under this category represent traits that, although usually assessed in only one restricted setting, are presumed to be characteristic of individuals across situations. Behaviors specific to the individual's relationships, such as marriage, as well as those related to sexual and sex-role functioning, will be discussed in the next section. Where studies have dealt with more than one type of psychosocial characteristic, only those aspects of functioning relevant to the present definition of personality will be explored at this point. The literature on personality has been primarily empirical in orientation. Thus the following presentation will include discussion of the relative adequacy of the studies, their results, and speculation on reasons for these findings.

Studies on personality have addressed such behavioral and attitudinal tendencies as dependence-independence, introversion-extroversion, aggressiveness-submissiveness, ability to delay gratification, locus of control, and preoccupation with loss. As can be seen in table 3–5, nine of the ten studies were found to be of relatively high methodological adequacy: two studies met criteria for level I, seven studies were rated at level II, and one study was assigned to level V. The level-I study conducted by Baggett (1967) utilized three matched groups of subjects who differed on parent variables. Two measurement instruments of proven reliability and validity for the study's purposes were employed, and characteristics of both the deceased parent and the family structure following the death were specified. The level-II studies were similar except for the omission of details about the deceased parent and the family. The other level-I study, carried out by Hetherington in 1972, provided even more detail about the current family functioning of adolescent girls, those who had either lost a father through death or divorce, and those whose families were intact. The author interviewed the girls' mothers to determine their level of functioning and, if they were widowed or divorced, their attitudes towards their former husbands. In contrast to the literature previously reviewed, there were no studies rated at levels III and IV, largely because of the relative adequacy of the outcome measures used. Only in the one level-V study (Jacobson and Ryder 1969), which was so rated because of the lack of a comparison group, was the method of measurement of undemonstrated validity and reliability. It should be noted that this piece of research, which found that men who were parentally bereaved early in life were immature and devoid of intimacy, was meant to be exploratory, conducted in order to determine future directions for investigation.

All of the research in this area was consistent in finding differences between those who had survived a parent's death during childhood and control subjects who had not had this experience. The number of studies on each topic is relatively small, limiting the extent to which generalizations to other groups may be made. However, where there have been multiple studies on a topic, results have been generally congruent.

Six of the nine levels-I and -II studies have been concerned with behavior that can be described at the most general level as lack of assertiveness. In two of the studies, Birtchnell (1975) and Hetherington (1972), females who had, during childhood, lost a parent through death were found to be more dependent than those from intact families. In Hetherington's study, in which female dependency behaviors were investigated, daughters of widows did not differ from daughters of divorcees on this variable. Birtchnell's study looked at adult psychiatric patients who had lost their mothers before age ten, while Hetherington assessed lower-middle-class adolescents. Hetherington's findings may have been age or social-class specific since, using older, higher-socioeconomic-status subjects, Hainline and Feig (1978) were unable to replicate these results. These researchers found no differences between subjects of different family backgrounds.

Related to the findings of these studies, have been the work of Baggett (1967), Felner, Stohlberg, and Cowen (1975), and Santrock and Wohlford (1970). Baggett, in his detailed study showed that male college students who had lost a father through death were more submissive than those with a father who was present during childhood. Felner, Stohlberg, and Cowen found five-to-ten-year-old boys and girls to be more withdrawn and anxious than controls. In Santrock and Wohlford's study, father-absent boys in the fifth grade were found to be less aggressive and also better able to delay gratification if the reason for absence was death rather than divorce.

Related to the findings on lack of aggressiveness or assertiveness as coping styles would seem to be the results of Parish and Copeland's (1980) study. These researchers found male college students whose father had died to be more externally oriented in terms of locus of control than were males and females from divorced families, males and females from intact families, and females who had lost a parent through death. The bereaved males perceived the courses of their lives as not being contingent upon their own behavior. This development would make intuitive sense, since these individuals certainly have witnessed and been affected by death as the ultimate expression of lack of control over one's destiny. While it is difficult to account for the sex difference on this variable, the external locus of control of males would appear to be consistent with the rather passive tendencies seen in males and females in the studies cited above. Those who do not feel in control of their lives would tend to behave accordingly: to depend on others and to lack initiative in their interactions. The suggestion made by studies noted in the previous section, that bereaved children become suicidally depressed adults, would

Table 3–5
Methodological Data and Adequacy Ratings of Empirical Studies on Personality Variables and Parent Death during Childhood

Reference	Subject	Comparison Group Present	Group Matching (sex, age, SES)	Specify Type Loss	Statistical Sign Test
Baggett (1967)	Home adjustment, submissiveness	X	Three groups of matched college students: father present, deceased father, father separation for other reasons.	X	X
Birtchnell (1975)	Dependency	X	Age-and-sex-matched in-patients.	X	X
Bluestein (1978)	Preoccupation with loss	X	School children matched on age and sex, SES and race.	X	X
Felner, Stolberg, and Cowen (1975)	Anxiety, withdrawal	X	Normal versus school-services referred children, matched on age, sex accounted for some school-SES match.	X	X
Hainline and Feig (1978)	Dependency, shyness	X	College-age women with intact families, divorced parents, deceased father; sex-age matched.	X	X
Haworth (1964)	Preoccupation with loss	X	Two clinic groups with an absent parent versus nonclinic institutionalized versus children from intact families. Age and sex matched.	X	X
Hetherington (1972)	Dependency, shyness	X	Compared adolescent girls from intact versus divorced versus father-deceased families, matched on age, sex, SES.	X	X
Jacobson and Ryder (1969)	Immaturity	No	—	X	No
Parish and Copeland (1980)	Locus of control	X	Undergraduate college students, sex accounted for.	X	X
Santrock and Wohlford (1970)	Aggression delay of gratification	X	Fifth grade boys from same school.	X	X

Outcome Measure/Outcome	Could Study Be Replicated?[a]	Time of Assessment Loss	Characteristics of Deceased Parent	Family Structure	Rating
Sentence completion and self-report inventory. Sex x personality characteristic differences.	X	Both specified	Sex specified	No father substitute	I
MMPI, age x characteristic, differences found.	X	Age at loss	NI	NI	II
Interpretation of tree drawings. Bereaved children more often perceive part of the tree as dead.	X	NI	NI	NI	II
AML checklist, teacher-referral form. Parent-death group more anxious, withdrawn.	X	NI	NI	NI	II
Structured observations and interviews. ND.	X	Age at assessment	Sex specified	NI	II
Rorschach, TAT—high reliability obtained. Higher loss scores and themes.	X	Both specified	Sex, number parents deceased	NI	II
Structured observations and interviews. Daughters of widows more shy, timid with males, dependent.	X	Age at assessment	Sex specified	Information about mother's behavior	I
Interview. Immaturity, lacking interpersonal competence.	Not easily	Age at loss	Sex specified	NI	V
Rotter internality-externality scale. Sex x loss differences on externality.	X	Age at assessment	Sex specified	NI	II
Gratification-delay task, doll play, interview. Differences on aggressiveness and delay of gratification.	X	Both specified	Sex specified	NI	II

also be consistent with both the presence of external locus of control and passivity. A major dynamic of depression is a feeling of helplessness, a belief that nothing one can do will positively affect one's situation.

The two remaining level-II studies (Bluestein 1978, Haworth 1964) deal with the preoccupation with loss and death among those who have experienced the death of a parent during childhood. Both of the studies, which assessed young children, showed that subjects did more often offer responses indicative of a concern with loss and death than did controls. One might speculate that these children might still be undergoing the mourning process, since the death must have been within a few years of assessment. Differential interpretation of results by the authors with respect to time of loss and time of assessment would be necessary in order to more fully understand the meaning of these findings.

In view of the fairly consistent positive results in relating personality variables to childhood bereavement of a parent, researchers should be encouraged to explore this area further. More research on such variables as locus of control and delay of gratification would further clarify earlier findings. Longitudinal research on these and other topics would also expand understanding of the consequences of this childhood experience. A follow-up on Hetherington's 1972 study, for example, showed that the behavioral tendencies observed in adolescence were consistent with the types of marital relationships these subjects developed (cited in Hetherington and Parke 1979). Finally, as in research on other topics in the field, future studies need to better account for the particulars on the subjects' experiences relative to characteristics of their family situations. When such information is provided, interaction among variables is often found. Specific information of this kind is necessary before appropriate generalizations of practical significance can be made.

Sex Role, Sexual, and Related Interpersonal Functioning

That interest in sex role, sexual, and related interpersonal functioning, as they pertain to parent-absence, particularly to father-absence has been strong can be concluded from the large number of studies on these related topics (reviewed by Biller 1971, 1974, 1981; Fulton and Markusen 1971; Herzog and Sudia, 1973). On the basis of both intuitive reasoning and the generalizations from research showing that parents serve as strong sex-role models for their children (for example, Bandura and Walters 1963), it has been assumed that absence of the parent of same sex or of two parents in a stable marital relationship, will be associated with problems in heterosexual functioning. Much of this research has dealt with children of divorced parents or with undifferentiated parent absence. The twelve studies that are concerned specifically with death of a parent will be critically reviewed in this section, and results will be compared with conclusions drawn by reviewers who examined the relationship between heterosexual functioning and parent absence in general.

Research in this area has focused on sex-role identification and behavior, marital relationships, heterosexual-interpersonal behavior, and sexual behavior. Table 3–6 summarizes methodological data and adequacy ratings on the empirical studies reviewed. As can be seen in this table and table 3–7, in which ratings of research by topic and outcome are presented, seven of the studies are relatively adequate in terms of methodology (levels I and II), while the remaining studies were rated lower because of procedural flaws. One level-III study was counted more than once, since it addressed both marital relationships and sex-role behavior. Differences between subjects who were parentally bereaved during childhood and those from other family backgrounds were found in eleven of the studies, including the study counted twice. All six of the relatively satisfactory studies resulted in positive outcomes. The four level-I studies were distributed among all of the topics but sexual behavior.

Sex-role identification and behavior were addressed in four studies, all of which yielded positive outcomes (Archibald et al. 1962; Baggett 1967; Clarke 1961; Martindale 1972). The procedures utilized in the one level-I study conducted by Baggett were described in the section on personality. Relevant to this section was his finding that college women whose fathers had died before they were eight were more traditionally feminine on a masculinity-femininity measure than were women who had grown up with their fathers in the home and women who had lost their fathers for other reasons before the age of eight.

The other highly rated study was Clarke's, assigned to level II because data about age at the time of loss and on family structure were omitted. Clarke (1961) found that all father-separated third-grade boys showed less traditional masculinity than those from intact families. Boys who had lost their fathers through death or who had experienced another form of complete separation scored lower in masculinity than did boys who had experienced intermittent father absence because of separation or divorce. The other two lower-rated studies (levels III and V) also showed that father-absent males presented less masculine behavior or identification than did controls.

Both the findings that father-absent girls show more traditional femininity and that father-absent boys show less traditional masculinity may be consistent with the findings of the previous two sections. Depression, passivity, dependency, and external locus of control, found to be char-

Table 3–6
Methodological Data and Adequacy Ratings on Empirical Studies of Sexual Identity, Behavior and Relationships, and Parent Death during Childhood

Reference	Subject	Comparison Group Present	Group Matching (sex, age, SES)	Specify Type Loss	Statistical Sign Test
Archibald et al. (1962)	Marital discord, sex-role disturbance	X	Compared VA-clinic patients with normative estimates of life insurance table. Demographics accounted for.	X	X
Baggett (1967)	Sex-role identification	X	Three groups of matched college students: father present, deceased father, father separation for other reasons.	X	X
Clarke (1961)	Sex-role identification	X	Age-matched boys separated from fathers for various reasons.	X	X
Earle and Earle (1959)	Marital discord	X	Age-and-sex-matched psychiatric inpatients.	NI	X
Gay and Tonge (1967)	Marital discord	X	Psychiatric inpatients. No controls or accounting for age, sex, SES.	X	No
Hainline and Feig (1978)	Interpersonal behavior with males	X	College-age women with intact families, divorced parents, deceased father. Age and sex matched.	X	X
Hetherington (1972)	Interpersonal behavior with males	X	Compared adolescent girls from intact versus divorced versus father-deceased families. Matched on age, sex, SES.	X	X
Hetherington and Parke (1979)	Marital adjustment	X	Follow up on 1972 study.	X	X
Illsley and Thompson (1961)	Marital adjustment	X	Normally distributed sample of maternity-hospital patients, hospitalized for birth of first child.	X	No percentages signif. figures for this project

Outcome Measure/Outcome	Could Study Be Repli- cated?[a]	Time of Assessment Loss	Charac- teristics of Deceased Parent	Family Structure	Rating
Case history. Difficulties in masculine identification with father loss. Depen- dency and hostility in marriage with mother loss.	X	NI	NI	NI	III
Sentence completion and self-report inventory. Sex by age-at-loss differences in sex-role identification.	X	Both specified	Sex specified	No father substitute	I
IT scale. Less masculinity for all father-separated boys, but more extreme for completely separated (death or other).	X	Age at as- sessment	Sex specified	NI	II
Interview data (divorce versus intact marriage) more broken marriages.	X	Age at loss	NI	NI	III
Case history ND with parent loss due to death (except both).	No	Age at loss	Sex specified	NI	IV
Structured observations and interview. ND.	X	Age at as- sessment	Sex specified	NI	II
Structured observations and interview. Anxiety and shyness in interacting with males.	X	Age at as- sessment	Sex specified	Detailed	I
Structured interview. Married vocationally successful and ambitious men who were overly controlled and inhibited.	X	Age at as- sessment	Sex specified	Detailed	I
Structured interview, self- report scales. Type loss by family-structure differences.	X	Both speci- fied	Detailed	Detailed	I

Table 3–6 Continued

Reference	Subject	Compari-son Group Present	Group Matching (sex, age, SES)	Specify Type Loss	Statistical Sign Test
Jacobson and Ryder (1969)	Marital adjustment	No —		X	No
Martindale (1972)	Cross-sexual identification	No —		Yes, but not dif-feren-tially related to findings	No
Moran and Abe (1969)	Homosexuality	X	Age-matched male psy-chiatric inpatients.	X	X

acteristic of individuals who had lost a parent through death would also be consistent with what has been considered feminine, and therefore less masculine, behavior. Comparisons of the instruments used to measure each of these behavior patterns would be necessary in order to further speculate on this connection. Also useful would be studies looking at mother loss and sex-role identification in order to determine whether the latter is influenced primarily by the father. Findings from the research reviewed above and those on father absence and the father's roles and their effects reviewed by Biller (1971 and 1974) and Lamb and Lamb (1976), do not necessarily exclude the mother's influence, since children who had lost mothers were not considered.

Two of the seven studies concerned with marital relationships were assigned a rating of level I. These studies revealed differences in characteristics of marital interactions involving those who were parentally bereaved early in life and marital patterns of nonbereaved controls. Three of the five remaining studies also had positive outcomes.

The follow-up on Hetherington's research of 1972 (cited in Hetherington and Parke 1979) was described in detail in the section on personality. In this study, structured interviews on marital choices and marital success of the now postadolescent subjects were conducted. The researchers found that daughters of widows, who were shy and dependent on females during adolescence, tended to marry vocationally successful and ambitious men who were socially inhibited and constricted. These paternally bereaved women contrasted with daughters of divorcees—more likely to be young and pregnant at marriage and to divorce or separate from their husbands, who had lower educational and vocational

Outcome Measure/Outcome	Could Study Be Replicated?[a]	Time of Assessment Loss	Characteristics of Deceased Parent	Family Structure	Rating
Interview. Sex by age-at-loss differences.	NI	Age at loss	Sex specified	NI	V
Listing in *Oxford Anthology of Verse*, life history, higher cross-sex identification.	Not easily	NI	Sex specified	N	V
Psychiatric diagnosis. ND.	X	NI	NI	NI	III

attainments and a higher rate of criminal activity than husbands of other subjects. Women from intact families were reported to have made the most realistic marital choices.

The other level-I study, carried out by Illsley and Thompson (1961), was an exhaustive investigation into the characteristics and consequences of broken homes. Illsley and Thompson assessed women who had been separated from a parent during childhood and were now giving birth to their first child. Age at separation, ordinal position, family size, sex of parent, type of separation and circumstances after the separation—such as economic changes and the presence of substitute parents—were considered in closely matching controls and subjects. Structured interviews emphasizing verifiable behaviors such as school attendance and time of pregnancy, and a validated adjustment-scale were used to measure differences among groups. It was found that women who had lost a parent for reasons other than death had lower-level jobs than bereaved women (as did their husbands) and were more likely to have conceived and delivered a child in their teens or before marriage. Those parentally bereaved subjects who were raised by their mother and a stepfather were more similar to those who were parent separated for other reasons, while parentally bereaved subjects raised within different family structures were most like controls raised in intact families. On the average, women who experienced any form of parent loss appeared less disturbed on a measure of adjustment to pregnancy and marriage than did women from intact families, although their scores tended to more extreme.

Two of the remaining studies found the parentally bereaved to have experienced marital problems (Earle and Earle 1959; Jacobson and Ryder

Table 3–7
Ratings of Studies on Sexual, Sex Role, and Heterosexual Interpersonal Functioning, by Topic and Outcome

Rating Outcome	I			II			III[a]			IV			V			Totals by disorder		
	+	–	Total	+	–	Total	+	–	Total	+	–	Total	+	–	Total	+	–	Total
Sex Role	1	0	1	1	0	1	1	0	1	0	0	0	1	0	1	4	0	4
Marital Relationships	2	0	2	0	0	0	2	0	2	0	1	1	1	0	1	6	0	6
Heterosexual interpersonal relationships	1	0	1	1	0	1	0	0	0	0	0	0	0	0	0	2	0	2
Sexual behavior	0	0	0	0	0	0	0	1	1	0	0	0	0	0	0	0	1	1
Totals by rating	4	0	4	2	0	2	3	1	4	0	1	1	2	0	2	12	1	3

[a]One level III study was counted more than once as it addressed 2 topics (marital and general sex role).

1969) while Gay and Tonge (1967) found differences only in those who had lost both parents to death.

Related to functioning-within-marriage is behavior specific to heterosexual relationships. Two studies, by Hetherington (1972) and Hainline and Feig (1978), rated at levels I and II respectively, were concerned with females' social functioning in the presence of males. Both of these studies have been described previously. Hetherington found adolescent girls to be shy with males, and to avoid eye contact and physical proximity with them. This behavior contrasted with that of subjects from families in which there was a divorce and from intact families. This behavior can again be considered consistent with the passivity and related patterns observed in other studies of bereaved children. Hainline and Feig, however, failed to obtain similar results in their study of college women. Their subjects were older and of higher socioeconomic status, and may have differed on variables related to their families but not described.

Only one study dealt with sexual behavior and sexual identification. This study, by Moran and Abe (1969) was rated at level III since psychiatric diagnoses were used to differentiate among subjects. No difference was found in the rate of homosexuality of parentally bereaved and other subjects.

Credible evidence thus exists for an association between parent bereavement in childhood and variations in the individual's later sex-role behavior, heterosexual social-functioning, and characteristics of marital relationships. Due to the small amount of research and the focus on groups of subjects and aspects of behavior that have been narrowly defined, generalizations cannot be made with confidence. Work on sex roles has tended to focus on young male subjects, while the literature on heterosexual social and intimate behavior, including marriage, has been concerned with females from adolescence on. Future research might look at the reverse, or at both sexes simultaneously in order to assess possible sex differences. Information about the sex of the deceased parent is especially important when researching this topic, as some of the investigators have recognized. Knowledge about the relationship between parent and child and about the personality characteristics of the deceased and surviving parent would also be necessary in attempting to support hypotheses about modeling. These variables will affect the extent to which children will imitate one parent or another. The age at which the loss takes place would also seem to affect sex-role identity and ease in relating to members of the other sex. In order to clarify these issues, longitudinal research, such as that carried out by Hetherington should be undertaken by more researchers. The research in this area has, in general, been of higher quality than on any other topic, but needs to be expanded in order to show more clearly the nature of the association between sex role and heterosexual social functioning and the death of a parent.

Conscience Development, Juvenile Delinquency, and Criminal Behavior

Reasoning about conscience development and delinquent and criminal behavior has been similar to that concerning sex role and heterosexual interpersonal functioning. It has been assumed that there will be problems without the modeling and guidance provided by parents, particularly fathers. Research on this topic has, again, dealt for the most part with general father or parent absence, and very few studies on parental bereavement were located. This section will begin with a brief review of the father-absence literature; analysis of the studies and review articles on death of a parent will follow.

Research has shown that father absence is more common among those who have engaged in delinquent and criminal behavior than among those who have not been involved in such activities (Biller 1971, 1974; Herzog and Sudia 1973). Herzog and Sudia have noted that the research may not reflect actual differences in behavior between the two groups. Policies among law-enforcement agencies on apprehending and reporting delinquency has been shown to vary with socioeconomic status (which is related to father absence) and with family structure. Lack of controls for socioeconomic status within the studies may have also affected the data according to these reviewers. Were the findings to be uncritically accepted, one hypothesis as to a cause for such results would be that antisocial behavior is expected of father-absent boys in much the same way as depression is expected of the parentally bereaved. Such expectations, which seem to be applied more to those whose fathers are absent for reasons other than death (less socially acceptable reasons), could result in a self-fulfilling prophesy: expected behavior will come to be realized.

Table 3–8 is a presentation of methodological data and adequacy ratings of empirical studies on associations between early parent death and conscience development, juvenile delinquency, and criminal behavior. The research was not easily categorized in terms of content or ratings. All of the studies utilized relatively valid and reliable outcome measures, and several contained much detailed information about the family and the deceased parent. Therefore the studies are of great descriptive value not reflected in the ratings assigned to them. Two problems led to low ratings in otherwise satisfactory research. One was the lack of statistical analyses of the data, an omission overlooked when sufficient information for determination of significance levels was provided. The other was the failure to differentially interpret results with respect to cause of parent absence.

None of the research on conscience development and absence of a parent focused specifically cn subjects who had lost a parent through death during childhood. One interesting and detailed study that may represent the parent-absence research at its best is that of Hoffman (1971). Adolescent father-absent and father-present subjects were matched on sex, age, IQ, socioeconomic status, ethnicity, and school grade. Father absence was defined as no adult male having lived in the home for six months prior to the study. Mothers' relationships with their children were analyzed, resulting in the finding that women without husbands expressed less affection towards their sons than those with husbands. Subjects were assessed on structured-projective measures, including sentence-completion tasks and responses to morality tales, as well as on ratings by parents, teachers, and peers on aggression, moral behavior, and attitudes. It was found that father-absent boys scored significantly lower than controls on moral judgment, guilt following transgressions, appropriate acceptance of blame, moral values, and rule conformity. They were also rated as more aggressive by teachers. No differences between father-present and father-absent girls were observed.

The failure to differentiate among subjects on the cause for father absence raises questions about interpretation of this data. Differences between children of divorced and widowed mothers on social and physical aggressiveness have been noted in studies cited previously. Santrock and Wohlford (1970) found that boys whose fathers were absent because of divorce were more aggressive than boys whose fathers had died. Similarly, Hetherington (1972) showed that daughters of divorcees, when compared to daughters of widows, were more socially aggressive with males. On the basis of this research one might speculate that Hoffman's sample was made up largely of children of divorced parents. The association between father absence and children's relationships with their mothers, which was in turn related to conscience development, might also be more finely differentiated through an analysis of the reason for separation from the father. Such a possibility would be suggested by the fact that divorced and widowed women have been found to differ with respect to their attitudes towards themselves and their former husbands, the degree to which they are concerned with their adequacy as mothers, and their perceptions about the quality of their relationships with their children (Hetherington 1972). Research modeled after Hoffman's study but with subjects differentiated as to reason for father absence would clarify these issues. Studies on mother absence would also be useful to verify or dispute the belief that fathers alone are instrumental in facilitating conscience development.

Six studies were located in which death of a parent during childhood

Table 3–8
Methodological Data and Adequacy Ratings on Empirical Studies of Associations between Early Parent Death and Conscience Development, Juvenile Delinquency, and Criminal Behavior

Reference	Subject	Comparison Group Present	Group Matching (sex, age, SES)	Specify Type Loss	Statistical Sign Test
Brown and Eppos (1966)	Prison sentences	X	Prisoners matched on all with normal controls.	X	X
Earle and Earle (1966)	Prison sentences	X	Psychiatric inpatients from intact and mother-absent families. Age and sex matched.	X	X
Glueck and Glueck (1950)	Juvenile delinquency	X	JD and controls matched on all.	X	No—easy to figure
Hoffman (1971)	Conscience development	X	Adolescent father-absent and-present groups, controlled on all.	No	X
Huttunen and Niskanen (1978)	Criminal record	X	Ss who lost their father prenatally compared with Ss who lost a father during first year, SES and age-controlled, sex accounted for.	X	X
Koller (1970)	Juvenile delinquency	X	Delinquent girls matched on all with normal controls.	X	No—not easy to figure on parent loss
Monahan (1957)	Juvenile delinquency	X	JD's of different family backgrounds no matching.	X	No—easy to find

was associated with delinquency or criminal behavior. The distribution with respect to methodological adequacy rating was as follows: level I—one study, level II—three studies, level IV—two studies. All of the research relied on court records of rates of delinquent and criminal activity or recidivism.

The level-I study, considered a classic in the field of juvenile delinquency, was conducted by Glueck and Glueck in 1950. Five-hundred

Outcome Measure/Outcome	Could Study Be Replicated?[a]	Time of Assessment Loss	Characteristics of Deceased Parent	Family Structure	Rating
Sentencing to prison. Higher percentage had lost a parent to death.	X	Age at loss	NI	NI	II
Incidence of prison sentences. Higher percentages bereaved had been parentally bereaved.	X	Age at loss	Sex specified	NI	II
Rate of JD (court records). Higher rate for paternally bereaved and for other father absent	X	Both specified	Sex specified	Detailed	I
Sentence completion, R's morality tales ratings by teachers, parents, peers. Sex x age x father-absence differences.	X	Both specified	Sex specified	Mother-child relationship described	V
Court records of criminal activity. Higher rates among those whose fathers died before their birth.	X	Both specified	Sex specified	NI	II
Sentencing to training school. Higher general-parent loss.	X	Both specified	Age and sex specified	Specified	IV
JD recidivism cases. High percentage father absence in general, ND between father death and intact family.	No	NI	NI	NI	IV

matched pairs of male juvenile delinquents and nondelinquent controls were assessed on father absence versus presence, and reasons for absence. Family size, level of living conditions, family cohesiveness and the degree to which mothers supervised the boys' activities were considered in the analysis. It was found that more than two fifths of the delinquent boys were father absent as compared with less than one quarter of the non-delinquent group. Twenty percent of the mothers of juvenile delinquents were widowed while only ten percent of the mothers of nondelinquents had lost their husbands through death.

Two of the level-II studies, which omitted family information, showed that parentally bereaved individuals were overrepresented among those sentenced to serve prison terms (Brown and Eppos 1966), Earle and Earle 1959). The other level-II study revealed that individuals whose fathers had died before their birth had higher rates of criminal activity than subjects whose fathers died during their first year of life (Huttunen and Niskanen 1978). The remaining two studies seemed to indicate that parent absence (other than parent death) was associated with juvenile delinquency (Koller 1970; Monahan 1957).

As this review and others (Brown and Eppos 1966; Epstein et al. 1975; Fulton and Markusen 1971) have indicated, preliminary research suggests that there may be a relationship between delinquent and criminal behavior and death of a parent. A connection between conscience development, which is presumably a precurser to socially acceptable or delinquent or criminal behavior, and childhood bereavement, as differentiated from parent absence in general, has yet to be shown in any study. Work specific to parentally bereaved subjects will provide further verification for the preliminary speculations that have been made.

One issue needing clarification is the seeming contradiction between the consistent evidence that individuals who, as children, lose a parent through death tend to be nonaggressive, and the possibility that this type of family background is also associated with delinquent and criminal tendencies. Several possible explanations might be applied, should these findings be further verified. Aggressiveness might be a dimension that is especially susceptible to change as a result of loss of a parent. Whether expression or constriction of aggressiveness is stimulated by a parent's death may depend on the nature of other situational or child-specific variables. An alternative hypothesis is that bereaved children are more passive and therefore more easily led by gangs involved in antisocial behavior. Differences in temperament between groups observed prior to bereavement would help to clarify this issue.

Cognitive, Academic, Scientific, and Creative Achievement

A small number of studies have been conducted on a variety of achievements of individuals who have experienced the death of a parent during childhood. The very existence of research in this area represents a marked departure from the orientation of most of the literature, which has been more negative in outlook, focusing on psychopathology, personality deficits, sex-role difficulties, and criminal behavior. Research on cognitive, academic, scientific, and creative achievement permits consideration of the possibility that "the bereavement process may be worked through in a constructive manner" resulting in increased motivation and energy to be applied towards creative accomplishment (Eisenstadt 1978). In this section, the seven studies and the related literature reviews and theoretical papers examining achievement in these areas will be critically reviewed.

Research on achievement, as on the last few topics reviewed, has been both sparse and fragmented. It has also been of relatively poor quality, as can be seen in table 3–9. Four of the eight studies were assigned a rating of V, two of level II, and one each of levels I and IV. In many cases the data has been derived from historical written accounts of famous persons, making it difficult to establish appropriate control groups. This problem was rather creatively addressed by Eisenstadt (1978), however. Other studies of live subjects have also omitted control groups and have in several cases utilized measurement techniques of questionable validity and reliability. The relatively adequate studies (Eisenstadt 1978; Lifshitz 1976; Santrock 1972) have shown that by using both historical records and more traditional methods, credible findings can be obtained.

Most of the work on cognitive and academic functioning has associated undifferentiated parent (usually father) absence with performance on these variables. One selective review article (Albert 1971) did examine cognitive development and bereavement, finding that early parentally bereaved children were overrepresented among groups of gifted individuals. Most researchers who have reviewed the literature have shown a relationship between father absence and deficits in cognitive and academic performance (Biller 1974, 1981; Herzog and Sudia 1973; Hetherington and Deur 1971; Shinn 1976). These authors have noted the existence of mediating factors such as socioeconomic status, race, amount of parent-child interaction, and anxiety, which affects the degree to which father-absent children differ from those from intact families on cognitive and academic performance.

Five studies that focused on parental bereavement and cognitive and academic success were located. Three of the studies were assigned a rating of level V, primarily because they lacked comparison groups. Two of these studies (Cox 1926, Hilgard, Newman, and Fisk 1960) associated loss of a father with high cognitive performance while the third showed a decline in academic achievement following parental bereavement (Kirkpatrick et al. 1965).

In one of the studies rated at level II, Lifschitz (1976), compared nine-to-fourteen-year old children whose fathers had been killed in an Israeli war three-to-six years prior to testing to children from intact fam-

Table 3–9
Methodological Data and Adequacy Ratings of Research on Childhood Parental Bereavement and Cognitive, Academic, Scientific, and Creative Achievement

Reference	Subject	Comparison Group Present	Group Matching (sex, age, SES)	Specify Type Loss	Statistical Sign Test
Cox (1926)	IQ	No		No	No percentages
Eisenstadt (1978)	Genius	Non-traditional	Encyclopedia-listed Ss compared with 1. split ½ 2. with fathers not listed 3. with base rates of parent death.	X	X
Hilgard, Newman, and Fisk (1960)	Academic success	No		X	No
Kirkpatrick et al. (1965)	Academic achievement	No		X	No
Lifshitz (1976)	Cognitive skills	X	Father bereaved versus not subjects sex, age, SES matched.	X	X
Martindale (1972)	Poetic eminence	No		Yes, but indiscriminately grouped	Percentages
Roe (1953)	Scientific achievement	X	Eminent scientists, versus college students no matching.	X	Percentages
Santrock (1972)	Academic, cognitive functioning	X	Matched on all for jr.-sr. high students from intact and father-separated families.	X	X

ilies. The subjects and controls were matched on all relevant variables and were assessed with structured observations, teacher ratings, and the Bieri test of cognitive complexity. Father-absent children were shown to be relatively deficient in cognitive skills defined as awareness and dif-

Outcome Measure/Outcome	Could Study Be Repli-cated?[a]	Time of Assessment Loss	Charac-teristics of Deceased Parent	Family Structure	Rating
Histories of parent loss in geniuses, as measured by IQ (retrospective). High per-centages early parent loss.	No	Historical retrospective	NI	NI	V
Listings of one column or more in *Encyclopedia Britannica* and *Encyclopedia Americana*. Overrepresenta-tion of loss of one or both parents.	X	Both specified	Sex specified	NI	I
Retrospective interview. Father absence associated with success in academic pursuits.	X	NI	Sex specified	NI	V
School records. Lowered achievement following a parent's death.	No		NI	NI	V
Bieri test of cognitive com-plexity structured observa-tions Teacher ratings. Age by father loss differences.	X	Both specified	Detailed	NI	II
Listing in *Oxford Anthology of Verse*, life history. Rela-tionship between general father loss and poetic emin-ence.	X	NI	Sex specified	NI	V
Listings of scientists, ac-counts of family back-ground. Overrepresentation of parent death by age 10.	Not easily	Age at loss	NI	NI	IV
Stanford Achievement Otis quick IQ. Age by type of loss differences.	X	Both specified	Sex specified	NI	II

ferentiation of environmental variables. Children who had lost a father before the age of seven scored lower on these measures of cognitive complexity than did subjects who had been older when their father died. The other level-II study (Santrock 1972) related scores on standardized achievement and intelligence tests to different types of father absence. Within the age-stratified sample, those who had become father-absent when they were between the ages of six and nine were found to score lower at ages eight and eleven than did control subjects from intact families. The most substantial differences were seen in children who had been separated from their fathers for reasons other than death.

Due to the small number of procedurally adequate studies concerned with different aspects of cognitive and academic functioning that have yielded disparate results, no conclusions concerning the relationship between cognitive and academic performance can be drawn. To develop this area more completely, there should be research to examine more of the cognitive and academic skills in verbal, performance, and quantitative areas. Relevant assessment measures of well-established reliability and validity are available for this purpose.

Three research reports were concerned with the relationship between genius and creativity and early death of a parent. Measures of these nebulous concepts were a prominent representation in encyclopedias, poetry anthologies, or listings of eminent scientists. All three of the studies, which were of varying quality (levels I, IV and V), showed that death of a parent occurred at a high rate in the background of these creative and gifted individuals.

The difficulty of finding controls appropriate for matching with subjects listed in texts (who were in many cases no longer alive) was dealt with in different ways by each of the researchers. Martindale (1972) omitted the use of controls entirely, thus limiting the extent to which findings from his study can be generalized. Roe (1953) compared her scientist subjects with college students, but because she did not document matching on such variables as age, sex, and social class, the control group served little purpose. Eisenstadt (1978) used three methods for placing data about his subjects, obtained from encyclopedia listings, in larger perspectives. He used a split-half reliability test on his group of subjects, compared the subjects with their eminent and less well-known fathers, and compared bereavement rates from census and insurance tables. Consistency in finding that loss of one or both parents occurred more frequently among subjects lent support to Eisenstadt's hypothesis concerning the association between parental bereavement and genius.

There is some research, then, showing associations between parental bereavement during childhood and both cognitive and academic deficits and exceptional performance in a variety of fields. Determining differences in the family and individual backgrounds of subjects would be necessary in assessing reasons for dissimilarities in levels of functioning. It may be, for example, that bereaved children who become high achievers have a surviving parent who is unusually involved or achievement oriented. Information about levels of performance before, as well as after, bereavement would help in appropriately attributing connections among variables.

There seem also to be contradictions between the research on creativity and genius and that on locus of control (Parish and Copeland 1980) cited earlier. It would seem that individuals with external locus of control would be much less likely to make exceptional achievements in science and the arts due to the drive and self-initiated energy necessary for such pursuits. Again, further investigation into individual and family characteristics might help in determining which individuals may be defeated by parental bereavement and which will be, in Albert's (1971) words, "cognitively freed."

Summary of Research on Behaviors Observed
Subsequent to the Death of a Parent

The preceding sections indicate that, with the exception of work on immediate reactions, empirical research of relatively high quality has been conducted on each group of behaviors observed subsequent to the death of a parent. However, as can be seen in table 3—10, fewer than half (40 percent) of all the studies rated met the standards for levels I and II. The proportions are approximately equivalent when studies that were rated more than once because they address more than one area of functioning are excluded (table 3–11). A high proportion of the studies showed that subjects bereaved of a parent in childhood differed from controls who had not had this experience: 81 percent of all studies and 77 percent of studies, when a correction was made for duplicates, yielded positive outcomes. Nearly all of the methodologically sound studies showed differences between bereaved subjects and nonbereaved controls.

From the review of the research on different categories of behaviors

Table 3–10
Ratings and Outcomes of Studies on Behaviors Observed Subsequent to the Death of a Parent

Level	+	−	Total
I	8	0	8
II	24	2	26
III	18	9	27
IV	7	5	12
V	12	0	12
Totals	69	16	85

Table 3–11

Ratings and Outcomes of Studies on Behaviors Observed Subsequent to the Death of a Parent, Corrected for Duplications[a]

Level	+	−	Total
I	6	0	6
II	21	2	23
III	17	9	26
IV	6	5	11
V	8	0	8
Totals	58	16	74

[a]Two studies which were rated twice (each was rated at levels II and III) are included at both levels. These studies employ a number of different measurement techniques to assess multiple areas of functioning, and each may appropriately be considered to represent two studies of different levels of adequacy.

observed subsequent to the death of a parent, it can be concluded that the evidence on differences between bereaved and nonbereaved individuals varies with the type of behavior being assessed. The data on immediate reactions to the death of a parent are exclusively descriptive and theoretical, and therefore cannot be interpreted with a high degree of confidence in reliability and validity. There are general indications that children do undergo a process of bereavement similar to that experienced by adults.

The highest proportion of the research is concerned with manifestations of emotional disturbance, and almost a third of these studies qualified for ratings of levels I and II. Most of this research yielded positive outcomes, and this was particularly true of the higher-rated studies. Subjects who had lost a parent were found to be overrepresented among those with symptoms of suicidal and, to a lesser extent, psychotic behavior, and among those judged as maladjusted on a more general basis.

Most of the few studies conducted on personality variables were found to be of relatively high quality. Most of the levels-I and -II studies showed that those who had lost a parent through death were more submissive, dependent, introverted, and preoccupied with loss than were those of different family backgrounds. They were also more likely to have an external locus of control.

Almost half of the studies on sex role, sexual, and heterosexual-interpersonal functioning were judged to meet the standards for levels I and II. These studies showed males score lower on measures of sex-role behavior and females appear more feminine than controls. The type of behavior represented by these measures is consistent with that found to be characteristic of subjects on personality measures. Parentally bereaved females were also found to have difficulty relating to males. Marital relationships were also found to differ, but not in terms of success or failure.

Conscience development was not explored specifically in relation to the experiencing of the death of a parent. Delinquent and criminal behavior was researched, and was shown to be associated with parent loss. Four of the seven studies on this topic were rated within the top two categories, and all resulted in positive outcomes.

The last category discussed was cognitive, academic, scientific, and creative achievement. Only three of the studies in this category were judged of relative methodological adequacy. One of the studies showed deficits in social-perception skills among the bereaved; another indicated relative cognitive and academic deficits in father-absent children as a group; while the third study found that those who had lost a parent during childhood were overrepresented among geniuses.

As was asserted repeatedly in these discussions, the choices of topics for research appear to have been logically guided by expectations of behaviors that might change as a result of parental bereavement during childhood. Thus, a variety of areas of functioning, such as athletic skills, parenting behavior, forms of emotional disorder (as paranoia, anxiety, character disorders and hyperactivity), substance addiction, and choice of career have not been investigated. It is clear that the field is in need of further development in terms of both the scope and technical quality of the research.

4

Family and Situational Variables Related to the Death of a Parent

In this section, the analysis of the literature focuses on variables within the child's environment that may influence the way in which a parent's death will affect him or her. These variables include aspects of the loss process: type of loss, preparation, and beliefs and rituals surrounding the death; characteristics of the deceased parent: sex, age, attitude towards dying, and relationship with the child; and factors specific to the family living situation before and after the death: family adjustment, climate, structure, religion, ethnicity, and socioeconomic status. Where empirical evidence exists, it is related to the various behavioral outcomes. There is also speculation about the role of less-well-researched variables.

Sex of the Deceased Parent

Death of the Father

The sex of a parent who dies would be expected to be an influential factor in what effects the death will have on the child's future adjustment and development. As has been discussed, mothers and fathers typically play different roles and fill different needs in the lives of their children and their deaths could not be expected to produce identical outcomes. A number of studies have not been sensitive to this possibility, and have treated children of deceased parents as a homogeneous group (Hilgard and Newman 1963). About half of the studies do differentially relate the sex of the deceased parent to later behaviors in children, however. These studies have either included children of deceased parents of both sexes and interpreted outcomes with consideration of these factors, or have only examined behaviors of children of either deceased mothers or fathers.

Most of the studies focusing specifically on the loss of parents of one sex, have been concerned with loss of the father. Several factors may have contributed to this emphasis. One is that fatherlessness is in fact a more prevalent condition since, at all ages, deaths of men are disproportionately high relative to deaths of women. In 1978, 3.5 percent of the child population was affected by the death of a father compared to the 1.4 percent experiencing a mother's death (U.S. Social Security Administration). In addition, the literature on parent death may have been influenced by the research on the effects of divorce on children. In this case, separation from the father is by far the more common experience. Ninety percent of the children whose parents are divorced live with their mother (Biller 1981). Research in which general parent absence or separation (for various reasons) has been investigated would necessarily focus on absence of the father. Finally, it may be that the greater interest, recently at least, in the influence of a father's death is in part due to the fact that most researchers in the social sciences are themselves male and presumably fathers or would-be fathers.

The analysis that follows will be concerned with research focusing specifically on the death of a father as well as on studies in which parent sex has been differentially related to outcomes. Relevant research in all

Table 4–1
Methodological Data and Ratings on Studies of Father Loss

Reference	Subject	Comparison Group Present	Group Matching (sex, age, SES)	Specify Type Loss	Statistical Sign Test
Archibald et al. (1962)	Emotional disturbance, masculine identification	X	VA-clinic patients compared with normative estimates of bereavement by life insurance company.	X	X
Baggett (1967)	Personality, sex-roles	X	Three groups of matched college students: father present, deceased father, father absent for other reasons.	X	X
Bendicksen and Fulton (1975)	Emotional disturbance	X	General bereaved population followed longitudinally. Matched on all.	X	X
Birtchnell (1966)	Emotional disturbance	X	Depressed and non-depressed state hospital inpatients matched for age before grouping.	X	X
Birtchnell (1970)	Emotional disturbance	X	Psychiatric inpatients compared with outpatient medical patients. Age matching, sex, SES accounted for.	X	X
Birtchnell (1972)	Emotional disturbance	X	Psychiatric inpatients compared with medical patients. Age matching, sex, SES accounted for.	X	X

of the areas of functioning previously considered will be discussed and integrated with the findings of other reviews.

Methodological data and ratings on studies considering the death of a father are summarized in table 4–1. A breakdown of research by topic and outcome (positive or negative) is presented in table 4–2. Also in table 4–2 are indications of studies in which differences in outcome were attributed specifically to absence of the father. As can be seen, of the forty-six studies (including six counted twice because functioning in two areas was examined), over half were rated in the two highest categories. Since specification of deceased-parent characteristics was one of the criteria for Level I, and one that functioned to lower the ratings of numerous studies, it would be expected that a relatively large proportion of level-

Outcome Measure/Outcome	Could Study Be Repli- cated?[a]	Time of Assessment Loss	Charac- teristics of Deceased Parent	Family Structure	Rating
MMPI, psychiatric diagnosis. Overrepresentation of bereaved in clinic population.[a]	X	Age at admission	Sex specified	NI	II
Sentence completion and self report inventory. Sex x age at loss differences.[a]	X	Both specified	Sex specified	Some informa- tion	I
Behavioral observations and ratings. Differences in middle age fewer than in childhood.	X	Both accounted for	Sex specified	NI	II
Psychiatric diagnosis. ND between groups; differences between severely and moderately depressed found, more mother death in severely depressed.	X	Age at loss	Sex specified	NI	III
Psychiatric hospital admission. Some differences (age x age at loss found).	X	Both specified	Sex specified	NI	II
Psychiatric diagnosis. Higher percentage depressed inpatients were parentally bereaved.[a]	X	Both specified	Sex specified	NI	II

Table 4–1 Continued

Reference	Subject	Comparison Group Present	Group Matching (sex, age, SES)	Specify Type Loss	Statistical Sign Test
Birtchnell (1975)	Emotional disturbance	X	Psychiatric inpatients of various diagnoses compared. Age and sex matched.	X	X
Brill and Liston (1966)	Emotional disturbance	X	Psychiatric inpatients compared. Age and sex matched.	X	X
Brown and Eppos (1966)	Prison sentences	X	Prisoners matched on all with normal controls.	X	X
Brown, Harris and Copeland (1977)	Emotional disturbance	X	Depressed and nondepressed inpatients, neurotic nonpatients and normals compared. All women, no other matching.	X	X
Cain and Fast (1965)	Emotional disturbance	X	Bereaved versus nonbereaved child clinic clients compared. Age and sex matched.	X	Percentages only (Figured for this analysis)
Clarke (1961)	Sex role	X	Age matched boys separated from fathers for various reasons.	X	X
Dennely (1966)	Emotional disturbance	X	Depressed psychiatric inpatients compared with 1921 census figures.	X	X
Eisenstadt (1978)	Genius	Nontraditional	Encyclopedia listed is compared: 1. split ½, 2. with fathers not listed, 3. with base rates of parent death.	X	X
Forrest, Fraser, and Priest (1965)	Emotional disturbance	X	Psychiatric versus general hospital patients. Age and sex differences accounted for.	X	X
Gay and Tonge (1967)	Depression, marital discord	X	Psychiatric inpatients. No matching.	X	No
Glueck and Glueck (1950)	JD	X	JD and controls matched on all.	X	No; easily figured

Outcome Measure/Outcome	Could Study Be Repli- cated?[a]	Time of Assessment Loss	Charac- teristics of Deceased Parent	Family Structure	Rating
MMPI and case histories. Sex *x* parent sex difference on dependency scale.	X	Age at death	Sex specified	NI	II
Inpatient admission. Only father loss for reasons other than death significant.	X	NI	Sex specified	NI	II
Sentencing to prison. Higher percent had lost a parent to death.	X	Age at loss	NI	NI	II
Psychiatric diagnosis. Age at loss *x* sex of parent differ- ences in depressed.	X	Both specified	Sex specified	NI	III
Intake data: psychiatric diag- noses ND in parent bereave- ment except in psychosis (more bereaved).[a]	X	Both speci- fied and dif- ferentially related	Sex specified	NI	II
IT scale. Less masculinity for all father separated but especially complete separa- tion.	X	Age at assessment	Sex specified	NI	II
Psychiatric diagnosis. Sex *x* sex of parent *x* age at loss differences.[a]	X	Age at loss	Sex specified	NI	III
Listing of one column or more in two encyclopedias. Overrepresentation of loss of one or both parents.[a]	X	Both specified	Sex specified	NI	I
Psychiatric diagnoses. Early parent death higher among the paranoid.	X	Age at loss	Sex specified	NI	III
Case history. Differences with loss of opposite sex parent.[a]	No	Age at loss	Sex specified	NI	IV
Rate of JD; court records. Higher rate for paternally bereaved and for other father absent.[a]	X	Both specified	Sex specified	Detailed	I

Table 4–1 Continued

Reference	Subject	Compari-son Group Present	Group Matching (sex, age, SES)	Specify Type Loss	Statistical Sign Test
Hainline and Feig (1978)	Interpersonal-heterosexual functioning, personality	X	College age women with intact families, divorced parents, deceased fathers. Age and sex matched.	X	X
Haworth (1964)	Preoccupation with loss	X	Two clinic groups with an absent parent versus nonclinic institutionalized versus children from in-tact families. Sex and age matched.	X	X
Hetherington (1972)	Interpersonal sex role behav-ior, personality	X	Adolescent girls from in-tact families or with father loss due to death or divorce.	X	X
Hetherington and Parke (1979)	Marital adjustment	X	Follow up on 1972 study.	X	X
Hilgard and Newman (1963)	Emotional disturbance	X	Three groups: schizo-phrenic inpatients, alco-holic inpatients. SES, sex; age-matched con-trols.	X	X
Hilgard, Newman and Fisk (1960)	Academic achievement	No	—	X	No
Hill (1969)	Suicide	X	Two groups of depressed inpatients, one suicidal, age controlled.	X	X
Hill and Price (1969)	Depression	X	Endogenous and reactive depressed inpatients com-pared, controlled for age.	X	X
Huttunen and Niska-nen (1978)	Emotional disturbance	X	Subjects who lost father prenatally compared with subjects who lost a father during first year, sex matched.	X	X
Illsley and Thompson (1961)	Marital adjustment	X	Normally distributed sample of maternity-hos-pital patients, hospital-ized for birth of first child.	X	No—per-centage sig-nificantly figured for this

Outcome Measure/Outcome	Could Study Be Replicated?[a]	Time of Assessment Loss	Characteristics of Deceased Parent	Family Structure	Rating
Structured observations and interview. ND.	X	Age at assessment	Sex specified	NI	II
Rorschach, TAT (high reliability obtained). All loss groups scored higher.	X	Both specified	Sex, number of parents deceased	NI	II
Structured interview and observation. Bereaved equals shy, anxious, dependent.	X	Age at assessment	Sex specified	NI	I
Structured interview. Married vocationally successful and ambitious men who were overly controlled.[a]	X	Age at assessment	Sex specified	Detailed	I
Psychiatric diagnosis. Significant differences in bereavement for schizophrenics.	X	Age at admission	Sex specified	NI	III
Retrospective interview. Father absence associated with success in academic pursuits.[a]	X	NI	Sex specified	NI	V
Suicide attempt, psychiatric diagnosis. Suicide attempts were common in depressed women who lost their fathers.	X	Age at loss	Sex specified	NI	III
Psychiatric diagnosis of different types of depression. Age at loss x sex differences found.[a]	No	Age at loss	Sex specified	NI	IV
Psychiatric diagnosis. Higher percentage schizophrenics lost father prenatally.[a]	X	Both specified	Sex specified	NI	III
Structured interview and self report scales. Type loss x family structure differences.[a]	X	Both specified	Detailed	Detailed	I

Table 4–1 Continued

Reference	Subject	Comparison Group Present	Group Matching (sex, age, SES)	Specify Type Loss	Statistical Sign Test
Jacobson and Ryder (1969)	Marital adjustment, immaturity	No	—	X	No
Kirkpatrick et al. (1965)	Emotional disturbance	No	—	X	No
Koller (1970)	Juvenile delinquency	X	Delinquent girls matched on all with normal controls.	X	No
Lifshitz (1976)	Cognitive skills	X	Father bereaved versus nonbereaved subjects. Sex, age and SES matched.	X	X
Martindale (1972)	Emotional disturbance, poetic eminence	No	—	Yes, but indiscriminates grouping	No percentages
Munro and Griffiths (1968)	Emotional disturbance	X	Psychiatric inpatients, outpatients and general hospital controls. Age and geography matched.	X	X
Parish and Copeland (1980)	Locus of control	X	Undergraduate college students. Sex accounted for.	X	X
Pitts et al. (1965)	Emotional disturbance	X	Affectively disordered inpatients. Age, sex, SES, and M.S. with medical patients.	X	X
Santrock (1972)	Cognitive, academic functioning	X	Junior-senior high school students from intact and father-separated families.	X	X
Santrock and Wohlford (1970)	Aggression gratification delay	X	Fifth grade boys from same school.	X	X
Trunnell (1968)	Emotional disturbance	X	Father-present, -absent clinic subjects, matched on age, SES.	No	X
Tuckman and Regan (1966)	Emotional disturbance	X	Age matching of children in parent-separated homes.	X	X

[a]Father-specific differences

Outcome Measure/Outcome	Could Study Be Repli-cated?[a]	Time of Assessment Loss	Charac-teristics of Deceased Parent	Family Structure	Rating
Interview. Immaturity, poor marital adjustment.[a]	No	Age at loss	Sex specified	NI	V
School records. Changes in level of adjustment follow.	No	Age at loss	Sex specified	NI	V
Sentencing to training school. Higher general parent loss, especially father.	X	Both specified	Age and sex specified	Specified	IV
Bieri test of cognitive complexity, structured observations, teacher ratings. Age x father loss differences.[a]	X	Both specified	Detailed	NI	II
Listing in *Oxford Anthology of Verse*, life histories.[a] Relationship between psychopathology and father.	X	NI	Sex specified	NI	V
Psychiatric diagnosis. Inpatient depressives showed excess maternal bereavement.	X	NI	Sex specified	NI	III
Rotter internality-externality scale. Bereaved showed external locus of control.[a]	X	Age at assessment	Sex specified	NI	II
Psychiatric diagnosis. ND.	X	NI	Sex specified	NI	III
Stanford Achievement Test, Otis Quick IQ. Age x type of loss differences.[a]	X	Both specified	Sex specified	NI	II
Gratification delay task; doll play interview. Differences on aggressiveness and gratification delay.[a]	X	Both specified	Sex specified	NI	II
Psychiatric diagnosis. Environmental factors x parent characteristics x individual characteristics, differences.[a]	X	Age at death	Detailed	Prior, subsequent family situation detailed	III
Clinic referral. More clinic referral problems in homes with separation and divorce.	X	NI	Sex specified	Speculation concerning	II

Table 4–2
Ratings of Studies on Father Death, by Topic and Outcome

Topic	I				II				III			
	+	−	Father specific	Total	+	−	Father specific	Total	+	−	Father specific	Total
Emotional disturbance	0	0	0	0	6	1	3	7	9	2	5	11
Personality	1	1	1	2	4	0	3	4	0	0	0	0
Sexual-social functioning	3	1	3	4	3	0	3	3	0	0	0	0
Delinquent criminal behavior	1	0	1	1	1	0	0	1	0	0	0	0
Cognitive-academic-creative functioning	1	0	1	1	2	0	2	2	0	0	0	0
Total, by rating	6	2	6	8	16	1	11	17	9	2	5	1

I studies would deal with the death of a father. Over three quarters of the levels I and II studies showing positive outcomes attributed differences between groups specifically to absence of the father. (Some of these studies also attribute differences specifically to mother loss.) In all, 65 percent of the studies that directly considered loss of the father through death revealed differences related to father absence.

In research dealing with emotional disturbance and father death, there were no studies rated level I, and seven studies rated level II. Three of these studies (Archibald et al. 1962; Birtchnell 1970; and Cain and Fast 1965) showed that death of a father was specifically associated with some manifestation of emotional disturbance. Archibald et al. compared the incidence of childhood bereavement among patients at a Veterans' Administration mental-health clinic with nominative estimates generated from life insurance company statistics. They found that loss of both the mother and the father was higher than would have been predicted. In Birtchnell's study, only patients who experienced death of a father during childhood were overrepresented among adult psychiatric inpatients, although there was also association between hospital admission and recent death of a mother. Cain and Fast (1965) examined a group of clinic outpatients and determined that a high percentage of those with psychotic symptoms had had a father who had committed suicide.

A small proportion of the research on emotional disturbance was

IV				V				Total, by Behavior			
+	−	Father specific	Total	+	−	Father specific	Total	+	−	Father specific	Total
2	0	2	2	2	0	1	1	19	3	11	23
0	0	0	0	1	0	1	1	7	0	6	7
1	0	1	1	1	0	1	1	8	1	8	9
0	0	0	0	1	0	1	1	3	0	2	3
0	0	0	0	2	0	2	2	5	0	5	5
3	0	3	3	7	0	6	7	42	4	41	46

concerned specifically with father absence, compared to research on other areas of functioning. This pattern may be the result of expectations of researchers, founded on empirical evidence, about the roles of mothers and fathers. While there is no direct data showing that fathers do not play a role in affective development (some of the better research, such as that by Baumrind in 1967, have looked at the effects of parents as a unit), research has shown fathers to be more involved and influential than mothers in other areas of functioning, such as sex-role development and cognitive functioning (Lamb and Lamb 1976; Lynn, 1976). On the other hand, mothers, as the primary caretakers early in life, have been traditionally expected to fill the nurturing role, and this relationship has been considered the basis for subsequent emotional development (for example, Rheingold 1956). A theoretical extension of this position, held by psychoanalytic writers and others who have drawn support from research on institutionalized children (Spitz 1946), has been that emotional disturbance is linked to maternal deprivation. These conclusion have, of course, been drawn from observations of parentally deprived children. This issue will be raised again in the discussion of death of a mother. From the father-absence literature in this review and others (Biller 1971, 1974, 1981; Herzog and Sudia 1973; Hetherington and Deur 1971), it can be stated that there is some evidence of a relationship between father absence and emotional disturbance.

The research on personality and parent death has generally been of relatively high quality, and these standards have been upheld in the research on paternal death. Six of the seven studies were rated within the two-highest categories, and four of these outcomes related specifically to death of a father. These studies represent most of those conducted on personality and parent death. Thus the outcomes obtained are relatively consistent with those discussed in the general personality section, showing paternally bereaved subjects more likely to be submissive (Baggett 1967) dependent (Hetherington 1972), low in aggression and able to delay gratification (Santrock and Wohlford 1970), and externally oriented in terms of locus of control (Parish and Copeland 1980). These behaviors appear to be sex-role related, fitting with the behavior typically expected of females. The outcomes of the levels I- and II-studies focusing on sex roles (Archibald et al. 1962; Baggett 1967; Clarke 1961) are also consistent with these findings, showing sex role difficulties in males who had lost a father through death. These findings would thus support research indicating the father's instrumental function in transmitting sex-role behavior (Biller 1974; Lamb and Lamb 1976; Lynn 1976.) The sex-role behavior of both males and females appears to be affected by death of a father; both become less traditionally masculine. It might be speculated that not only does the father instill notions of sex-role behavior in his offspring of both sexes, but also that his modeling of traditionally masculine behavior is adopted to some extent by both his sons and daughters.

Other research on sex role and heterosexual-social relations has shown paternally bereaved females to be more anxious and shy with males than were those from other family backgrounds (Hetherington 1972) and to marry vocationally successful but affectively constricted men (cited by Hetherington and Parke 1979). Again, this behavior is consistent with the nonassertive style described in other studies. Illsley and Thompson (1961), in contrast, found differences specific to death of a father only in women who were raised by their mother and a stepfather (and thus might not be considered father absent). These subjects showed less conforming nonassertive behavior. Compared to those from intact families, they left school earlier and were more likely to conceive or deliver a child in their teens or before marriage. It is possible that, were other researchers to examine family-structure variables as carefully as did Illsley and Thompson, differences among those of different background would be found. It should be noted that Hetherington did control for these variables, but her findings are not necessarily inconsistent with those of Illsley and Thompson since she considered only subjects with no adult male living in the home.

The sex-role-related literature reviewed above was similar to the personality research not only in subject matter and outcome but in methodological adequacy and proportion of outcomes which could be attributed to paternal death. Seven of the nine studies considering death of a father were rated at levels I and II and, in six of these, absent-father-specific results were found.

Only three studies within the relatively sparce research of delinquent and criminal behavior considered father death specifically, and two of these were rated the top-two categories. Differences specifically attributable to father death were found in the one level I study by Glueck and Glueck (1950). They found that father absent boys, including those who were paternally bereaved were overrepresented among juvenile delinquents. Brown and Eppos (1966) found father absence, including paternal bereavement, to be characteristic of the backgrounds of both male and female prison inmates. More current research would be necessary before generalizations on a relationship between death of a father and delinquent behavior can be made.

All studies considering cognitive, academic and creative, functioning and paternal bereavement showed that differences could be attributed to loss of the father, rather than loss of mother or the loss or either parent. Three of these studies have shown relationships between father absence and genius, while one links father-absence to deficits in cognitive-and achievement-test performance in boys (Santrock 1972); and in the latter study, absence due to death was found to be less detrimental than absence due to divorce, separation, or desertion. Death of the father was most closely associated with poor scholastic functioning if it occurred when the boys were between six-and-nine- years of age. In Lifshitz's study, infancy through age seven was the critical period for paternal bereavement. The three studies are thus contradictory, suggesting that paternal bereavement may be either an asset or a liability to achievement. Investigations into the variable which could potentially cause these dichotomized outcomes, such as temperament, prior functioning, and the mother-child relationship, are needed.

The relationship between father absence in general and cognitive and academic difficulties has been noted by a number of reviewers (Biller 1971, 1974, 1981; Hamilton 1977; Herzog and Sudia 1973; Pedersen 1976; Shinn 1976). These authors have criticized much of the research for failing to consider the socioeconomic status of the subjects, a variable directly correlated with both cognitive-academic performance and father absence. The studies discussed above controlled for socioeconomic status.

Another factor, relevant both to cognitive-academic functioning and, quite probably, all other categories of behavior, is the nature of the mother-child relationship. Biller (1972) showed that a mother's negative attitude towards an absent husband (and men in general) was related to academic underachievement in boys. Overprotective or rejecting mothers in single-parent households were found to have sons with low self-concepts. Other writers have suggested similar relationships (Lynn 1974, Shinn 1976). It has been shown that a mother's behavior toward her children varies with temporary absences of her husband (Marsella, Dubanaski, and Mohns 1974). The effects of a father's death on his spouse, therefore, merits further exploration. Lynn (1974) and others have reasoned that it is easier for mothers to feel positive about a deceased husband than about a divorced husband. This tendency was demonstrated by Hetherington (1972). It is evident that a clear understanding of the effects of a parent's death requires exhaustive investigations of the family background of subjects.

Death of the Mother

In the last section, there was discussion of the proportionately few studies on death of the mother, compared to studies on death of the father, and

Table 4–3
Methodological Data and Ratings on Studies of Death of the Mother

Reference	Subject	Comparison Group Present	Group Matching (sex, age, SES)	Specify Type Loss	Statistical Sign Test
Archibald et al. (1962)	Emotional disturbance	X	Compared VA-clinic patients with normative estimates of bereavement by life insurance company.	X	X
Barry and Lindemann (1960)	Emotional disturbance	X	Psychiatric inpatients compared with normative estimates of bereavement from life insurance tables.	X	X
Bendiksen and Fulton (1975)	Emotional disturbance	X	General bereaved population followed longitudinally. Matched on all.	X	X
Birtchnell (1966)	Emotional disturbance	X	Depressed and non-depressed state-hospital inpatients matched for age before grouping.	X	X

of the possible reasons for this emphasis in the literature. The higher proportion of work on paternal bereavement in areas other than emotional disturbance was also noted and discussed. Earlier in this century, more research dealt with maternal deprivation, which referred to everything from psychological rejection of the child by the mother to lack of involvement of any caring adult (as in institutionalized children). Recent research has tended to identify reasons for deprivation more specifically and concretely. This section will analyze the studies that have included children of deceased parents of both sexes and have attempted to differentially relate outcomes to sex of parent, as well as the studies focusing on maternal death alone. Perhaps because of the relative dearth of research, no literature reviews on maternal bereavement were located, and thus there can be no comparisons with the conclusions of other authors.

Methodological data and ratings on studies of maternal bereavement are presented in table 4–3, and ratings by topic and outcomes were tabulated for table 4–4. It shows half as many studies conducted on death of a mother as on death of a father.

Three studies looked only at death of the mother, and all of these

Outcome Measure/Outcome	Could Study Be Replicated?[a]	Time of Assessment Loss	Characteristics of Deceased Parent	Family Structure	Rating
MMPI, psychiatric diagnosis. Overrepresentation of parentally bereaved in clinic population.[a]	X	Specifies age at admission	Sex specified	NI	II
MMPI. Psychiatric diagnosis. Overrepresentation of parentally bereaved.	X	Differentiated by time of loss	Sex specified	NI	III
Behavioral observations and ratings. Some differences (depression) seen in middle age, fewer than in childhood.[a]	X	Both accounted for	Sex specified	NI	II
Psychiatric diagnosis. ND between groups. Differences between severely and moderately depressed found, more mother death in severely depressed.	X	Differentiated by age at loss	Sex	NI	III

Table 4–3 Continued

Reference	Subject	Comparison Group Present	Group Matching (sex, age, SES)	Specify Type Loss	Statistical Sign Test
Birtchnell (1970)	Emotional disturbance	X	Psychiatric inpatients compared with outpatient medical patients. Age, sex matching, SES accounted for.	X	X
Birtchnell (1972)	Emotional disturbance	X	Psychiatric inpatients compared with outpatient medical patients. Age matching, Sex, SES accounted for.	X	X
Birtchnell (1975)	Emotional disturbance	X	Psychiatric inpatients of various psychiatric diagnoses compared. Age, sex matching.	X	X
Brown and Eppos (1966)	Prison sentence	X	Prisoners matched on all with normal controls.	X	X
Brown, Harris, and Copeland (1977)	Emotional disturbance	X	Depressed and non-depressed inpatients neurotic nonpatients, and normals compared. All women, no other matching.	X	X
Bunch et al. (1971)	Emotional disturbance	X	Suicides matched with controls on all.	X	X
Cain and Fast (1965)	Emotional disturbance	X	Bereaved versus non-bereaved child: clinic clients compared. Age and sex matched.	X	Percentages only (Figured for this analysis)
Dennehy (1966)	Emotional disturbance	X	Depressed psychiatric inpatients compared with 1921 census figures.	X	X
Earle and Earle (1959)	Emotional disturbance	X	Psychiatric inpatients from intact and mother absent families. Age and sex matched.	X	X
Forrest, Fraser, and Priest (1965)	Emotional disturbance	X	Psychiatric versus general hospital patients. Age and sex differences accounted for.	X	X
Gay and Tonge (1967)	Depression. Marital discord	X	Psychiatric inpatients. No matching.	X	No

Outcome Measure/Outcome	Could Study Be Repli- cated?[a]	Time of Assessment Loss	Charac- teristics of Deceased Parent	Family Structure	Rating
Psychiatric hospital admission. Some differences, age x age at loss differences found.	X	Both specified	Sex specified	NI	II
Psychiatric diagnosis. Higher percentage depressed inpatients were parentally bereaved.[a]	X	Both specified	Sex specified	NI	III
MMPI and case histories. Sex x parent sex, difference on dependency score.[a]	X	Age at death	Sex specified	NI	II
Sentencing to prison. Higher percentage had lost a parent to death.[a]	X	Age at loss	NI	NI	II
Psychiatric diagnosis. Age at loss x sex of patient differences in depressed.[a]	X	Both specified	Sex specified	NI	III
Actual suicide. Higher percentage male suicides had been maternally bereaved.[a]	X	Both specified	Sex specified	NI	II
Intake data, psychiatric diagnosis. ND in parental bereavement except in psychosis (more bereaved).	X	Both specified as well as time in between	Sex specified	NI	II
Psychiatric diagnosis. Sex x sex of parent x age at loss differences.[a]	X	Age at loss	Sex specified	NI	III
Psychiatric diagnosis. Depression more common in maternally deprived.[a]	X	Age at loss	Sex specified	NI	III
Psychiatric diagnosis. Early parent death higher among the depressed.[a]	X	Age at loss	Sex specified	NI	III
Case history. Differences with loss of opposite sex parent.[a]	No	Age at loss	Sex specified	NI	IV

Table 4–3 Continued

Reference	Subject	Comparison Group Present	Group Matching (sex, age, SES)	Specify Type Loss	Statistical Sign Test
Haworth (1964)	Preoccupation with loss	X	Two clinic groups with an absent parent vison clinic institutionalized children from intact families. Sex and age matched.	X	X
Hilgard and Newman (1963)	Emotional disturbance	X	Three groups: schizophrenic inpatients, alcoholic inpatients, and SES. Sex age, matched controls.	X	X
Hill (1969)	Suicide	X	Two groups of depressed inpatients, one suicidal. Controlled for age.	X	X
Hill and Price (1969)	Depression	X	Endogenous and reactive depressed inpatients compared. Controlled for age.	X	X
Illsley and Thompson (1961)	Marital adjustment	X	Normally distributed sample of maternity hospital patients hospitalized for birth of first child.	X	No percentages figured
Kirkpatrick et al. (1965)	Emotional disturbance	No		X	No
Koller (1970)	Juvenile delinquency	X	Delinquent girls matched on all with normal controls.	X	No
Munro and Griffiths (1968)	Emotional disturbance	X	Psychiatric inpatients, outpatients, and general hospital controls. Age, geographic location matched.	X	X
Pitts et al. (1965)	General emotional disturbance	X	Affectively disordered inpatients matched on age, sex, SES, and marital status with medical patients.	X	X
Wilson, Alltop, and Buffaloe (1967)	Emotional disturbance	X	Consecutively admitted depressed inpatients who were from intact or parent death families.	X	X

NI = no information provided

[a]Mother-absence specific difference

Outcome Measure/Outcome	Could Study Be Replicated?[a]	Time of Assessment Loss	Characteristics of Deceased Parent	Family Structure	Rating
Rorschach, TAT. High reliability obtained. All loss groups scored higher.	X	Both specified	Sex, number of parents deceased	NI	II
Psychiatric diagnosis, significant differences for schizophrenics.[a]	X	Age at admission	Sex specified	NI	III
Suicide attempt, psychiatric diagnosis. Suicide attempts more common in depressed women who lost fathers.	X	Age at loss	Sex specified	NI	III
Psychiatric diagnoses of different types of depression. Age at loss *x* sex differences found.	No	Age at loss	Sex specified	NI	IV
Structured interview and self-report scales. Type loss *x* family structure differences.	X	Both specified	Detailed	Detailed	I
School records. Changes in level of adjustment follow.	Not easily	Age at loss	Sex specified	NI	V
Sentencing to training school. Higher general parent loss especially father.	X	Both specified	Age and sex specified	Specified	IV
Psychiatric diagnosis. Inpatient depressives showed excess of maternal bereavement.[a]	X	NI	Sex specified	NI	III
Psychiatric diagnosis. ND.	X	NI	Sex specified	NI	III
Psychiatric diagnosis. MMPI. Parentally bereaved had higher scores on the psychotic tetrad.[a]	X	NI	Sex specified	NI	III

Parental Death and Psychological Development

Table 4–4
Ratings of Studies of Maternal Bereavement, by Topic and Outcome

Topic	I				II				III			
	+	−	Mother specific	Total	+	−	Mother specific	Total	+	−	Mother specific	Total
Emotional disturbance	0	0	0	0	5	0	3	5	11		11	11
Personality	0	0	0	0	1	0	0	1	0	1	0	1
Sexual-social functioning	1	0	0	1	0	0	0	0	0	0	0	0
Delinquent criminal behavior	0	0	0	0	0	0	0	0	0	0	0	0
Cognitive-academic-creative functioning	0	0	0	0	0	0	0	0	0	0	0	0
Total, by rating	1	0	0	1	6	0	3	6	11	1	11	12

were level-III studies on emotional disturbance. One study was counted twice since it dealt with both depression and marital discord. Fewer than one-third of the studies were rated within the top-two categories, as compared with over half of the research on father death. Within levels I and II, three-fifths of the studies resulted in outcomes that could be attributed to death of a mother (all within level II), while just over two-thirds of the father-death studies had similar results. Approximately the same proportion of mother- and father-death research led to findings that could be specifically attributed to the parent of the sex being examined.

The majority of the studies linking maternal bereavement with subsequent behaviors focused on emotional disturbance. Of the studies on topics other than emotional disorders, one each was categorized at level I and level II; absent-mother-specific outcomes obtained in neither. Most of the lower-level studies did attribute differences directly to the mother's death, but these findings cannot be interpreted with confidence.

Nineteen of the twenty-four studies on maternal bereavement were concerned with emotional disturbance, and fifteen of these (79 percent) yielded outcomes linked to maternal bereavement as separate from death of either parent or death of the father. This finding contrasts with the data on paternal bereavement in which half of the twenty-two studies on emotional disturbance showed absent-father-specific differences. Even fewer studies (three of eight) of relative methodological adequacy showed

IV				V				Total, by Behavior			
+	−	Mother specific	Total	+	−	Mother specific	Total	+	−	Mother specific	Total
1	0	0	1	2	0	1	2	19		15	19
0	0	0	0	0	0	0	0	1	1		2
0	0	0	0	1		1	1	2		1	2
1	0	0	1	0	0	0	0	1	0	0	1
0	0	0	0	0	0	0	0	0	0	0	0
2	0	0	2	3	0	2	3	23	1	16	24

a direct relationship with father death. Of the level-II studies on emotional disturbance and maternal death, three of the six associated outcomes specifically with death of the mother. These studies were conducted by Archibald et al. (1962), Bendicksen and Fulton (1975), and Birtchnell (1975). Both Archibald al. and Birtchnell showed that, among psychiatric inpatients, those who had lost a mother through death during childhood showed more psychopathological dependency. In the study by Archibald study, this observation applied to males who had lost a mother during childhood, while Birtchnell related this finding to women who were maternally bereaved before ten. Bendicksen and Fulton found some general symptoms of maladjustment in subjects who had been parentally bereaved of during childhood. The differences between those who had lost a parent and matched controls persisted, but in decreasing intensity, through early middle-age.

There is, then, the suggestion of a link between maternal bereavement and the development of emotional disturbance, a relationship that may be stronger than that between paternal bereavement and emotional disorders. More methodologically sound work on possible associations is needed to assess the validity of what is now speculation. It should be noted that death of a mother may be generally less traumatic than death of a father because because, due to the mother's usually larger role in child care, a mother-surrogate is more likely to be sought. Were a connection between maternal bereavement and emotional disturbance established, it would be interesting to determine whether changes in the roles of mothers and fathers have an effect on the apparent deprivation of motherless children. In the past, such children were unlikely to be cared for and nurtured primarily by their fathers (Ferri 1973). If fathers are now more likely to assume the major responsibility for nurturing and caretaking, a decline in the negative effects of maternal bereavement might be expected.

Reason for the Parent's Absence

Differences in the Experience of the Child with Death and Divorce

A large portion of the literature on the general topic of parent absence has not differentiated subject groups on the basis of the reason for separation. Most of this research was eliminated from this analysis because of the belief that the diverse reasons for parent loss: death, divorce, separation, desertion, absence due to military service or other employment factors, and removal by child-protective authorities due to neglect or abuse, represent separate and unique experiences and must be treated as such. Some researchers have recognized these differences and have included in their studies only subjects who have experienced the most common forms of parental absence, death, separation, and divorce. Outcome variables on both groups have been compared, and differences in behavior patterns have been discovered. In the discussion that follows, this literature will be critically reviewed, and the views of other writers on the way in which divorce and parent death are experienced by children will be presented.

The reasons for the absence of a parent hold distinct significance in the contexts of both society and the family. The way in which others behave toward these children and the expectations of the children's own behavior may differ. They are likely to behave in a sympathetic manner toward bereaved children, a response that may persist for many years after the death. Depression is often expected of bereaved children, and such an expectation may become a self-fulfilling prophesy. In general, others may be willing to excuse maladaptive behavior in children who have lost a parent through death, attributing such behavior to the children's presumably traumatic experience.

The treatment accorded to children of divorce may be quite different. There is still some stigma attached to divorce that may be reflected in the reactions of others toward the children of divorced parents. These children are less often expected to mourn the loss of a parent; instead, some form of acting-out behavior may be seen as consistent with their family backgrounds. The attribution of blame for behavior problems may be more of an issue in this situation and, while the parents are likely to be the recipients of such attitudes, the children will inevitably be effected.

Within the family, similar differences in behaviors and attitudes specific to the reason for parent absence may be manifested. It has been the consensus of many authors who have reviewed the father-absence literature that loss of a husband through death is less damaging to a woman's self-esteem than is divorce, and that a mother's treatment of her children will vary accordingly (Benson 1968; Biller 1971, 1981; Lynn 1974). A divorced mother is more likely to speak disparagingly about the father of her children and such an attitude has been associated with poor self-concept and acting-out in boys (Benson 1968, Lynn 1974). These authors have also stated that mothers find death easier to explain than divorce, and that young children find death less difficult to understand and accept. Although children may tend to blame themselves for any type of parent loss, such thoughts may seem more logical when a parent's leaving is clearly intentional. Differential reactions to the reasons for a mother's absence would be expected to be similar to reactions to a father's absence. While children of bereaved parents would, on the basis of this discussion, be expected to have an advantage over children of divorce, some aspects of adjustment might be easier for the latter. For example, Bowerman and Irish (1962) found that adjustment of children to stepparents was more satisfactory after a divorce, since the children were less likely to compare their parents' new spouses unfavorably with the absent parents. A parent absent due to divorce is less often idealized than is a deceased parent.

Fifteen studies were located that compared subjects who had lost a parent through death and through divorce. Methodological data and ratings on the research are presented in table 4–5. All but one of these studies yielded outcomes showing differences between subjects who had lost parents for different reasons. The breakdown of ratings was level I—three studies; level II—eight studies (one negative); level III—two studies; and level IV—two studies. Research was conducted on the relationship between different forms of parent absence and emotional disturbance, cognitive and academic functioning, personality, sex role and heterosexual-interpersonal behavior, and juvenile delinquency. There were studies categorized within levels I and II in all of these areas except juvenile delinquency.

Two level-II studies dealt with emotional maladjustment and parent loss. Tuckman and Regan (1966), in examining the backgrounds of children admitted to a mental-health clinic, found an overrepresentation of children who had lost a parent through separation or divorce, but not through death. Felner, Stolberg, and Cowen (1975) studied school chil-

Table 4–5

Methodological Data and Ratings of Research Comparing Children of Divorce and Bereavement

Reference	Subject	Compari-son Group Present	Group Matching (sex, age, SES)	Specify Type Loss	Statistical Sign Test
Clarke (1961)	Sex role	X	Age-matched boys separated from fathers for various reasons.	X	X
Crook and Raskin (1975)	Emotional disturbance	X	Depressed inpatients with suicidal attempts compared with nonsuicidal depressed subjects and normals, matched on sex and age.	X	X
Earle and Earle (1959)	Emotional disturbance	X	Psychiatric inpatients from intact and mother-absent families, age and sex matched.	X	X
Felner, Stolberg, and Cowen (1975)	Emotional disturbance	X	Normal versus school-referred maladapted children. Matched on age and sex, SES equivalent.	X	X
Hainline and Feig (1978)	Interpersonal heterosexual-functioning personality	X	College-age women with intact families, divorced parents, deceased fathers, age and sex matched.	X	X
Haworth (1964)	Preoccupation with loss	X	Two clinic groups with an absent parent versus now clinic institutionalized versus children from intact families, age and sex matched.	X	X
Hetherington (1972)	Interpersonal sexual behavior personality	X	Adolescent girls from intact families or with father loss due to death or divorce.	X	X
Illsley and Thompson (1961)	Marital adjustment	X	Normally distributed sample of maternity hospital patients, hospitalized for birth of first child.	X	No percentages given were figured for this
Hetherington and Parke (1979)	Marital adjustment	X	Follow up on 1972 study.	X	X

Outcome Measure/Outcome	Could Study Be Repli-cated?[a]	Time of Assessment Loss	Charac-teristics of Deceased Parent	Family Structure	Rating
IT scale. Less masculinity for all father separated but especially complete separa-tion.	X	Age at assessment	Sex specified	NI	II
Psychiatric diagnosis case histories of attempts. More parent loss among suicidal except for loss through death.	X	Age at loss	NI	NI	III
Psychiatric diagnosis. Depression more common in maternally deprived.	X	Age at loss	Sex specified	NI	III
AMI checklist, teacher refer-ral form. Bereaved group: More anxious, depressed, withdrawn.	X	Both specified	NI	NI	II
Structured observations and interview. ND.	X	Age at assessment	Sex specified	NI	II
Rorschach, TAT (high reliability obtained). All loss groups higher.	X	Both specified	Sex, number of par-ents de-ceased	NI	II
Structured interview and ob-servation. Bereaved equals shy, anxious dependent.	X	Age at assessment	Sex specified	NI	I
Structured interview and self report scales. Type loss x family structure differences.	X	Both specified	Detailed	Detailed	I
Structured interview. Mar-ried vocationally successful and ambitious men who were overly controlled, in-hibited.	X	Age at assessment	Sex specified	Detailed	I

Table 4–5 Continued

Reference	Subject	Comparison Group Present	Group Matching (sex, age, SES)	Specify Type Loss	Statistical Sign Test
Koller (1970)	Juvenile deliquency	X	Delinquent girls matched on all with normal controls.	X	No
Munro (1966)	Emotional disturbance	X	Depressed inpatients and age and sex matched general hospital controls compared.	X	X
Parish and Copeland (1980)	Personality	X	Undergraduate college students, sex accounted for.	X	X
Santrock (1972)	Cognitive, academic functioning	X	Jr. Sr.-high-school students from intact and father-separated families.	X	X
Santrock and Wohlford (1970)	Aggression gratification delay	X	Fifth grade boys from same school.	X	X
Tuckman and Regan (1966)	Emotional disturbance	X	Age matching of children in parent separated homes.	X	X

dren from intact families and from families in which a parent was absent due to death, divorce, or separation. They found that parent-separated children scored higher on a scale of maladjustment than did children from intact families. Subjects who had lost a parent through death were more anxious, depressed, and withdrawn than matched controls, while children whose parents were divorced or separated were more aggressive and tended to act-out. There were no prior differences in adjustment levels of the subjects and controls. The two studies appear to be contradictory, although it should be noted that children showing the behaviors Felner, Stolberg, and Cowen (1975) found in the bereaved groups are probably less likely to be referred to clinics, as these passive behaviors are less noticeable and less troublesome to those in a position to make clinic referrals, for example, teachers (see McCandless 1967).

One level-II study (Santrock 1972) dealt with cognitive and academic achievement. Santrock found depressed intelligence-and achievement-test scores among boys whose fathers were absent for any reason. Differences

Outcome Measure/Outcome	Could Study Be Repli-cated?[a]	Time of Assessment Loss	Charac-teristics of Deceased Parent	Family Structure	Rating
Sentencing to training school. Higher general parent loss, especially father.	X	Both specified	Ages, sex specified	Specified	IV
Psychiatric diagnosis severe versus moderate depression. ND between groups re: different types of loss.	No	NI	Quality of relationship with deceased parent, sex	NI	IV
Rotter internality-externality scale. Sex x reason for loss differences on gratification delay.	X	Age at assessment	Sex specified	NI	II
Stanford Achievement Otis Quick IQ. Age x type of loss differences.	X	Both specified	Sex specified	NI	II
Gratification delay task, doll play, interview. Differences on aggressiveness and gratification delay.	X	Both specified	Sex specified	NI	II
Clinic referral. More clinic referral problems in homes with separation and divorce.	X	NI	Sex specified	Specula-tion concerning	II

from controls who came from intact families were greatest for subjects who were father-separated for reasons other than death. Age at the onset of father absence was also a significant outcome factor.

With respect to personality variables, there were three level-II studies that compared children from a variety of family backgrounds. Differences between children who had lost parents for different reasons were found only in children who had lost both parents in Haworth's (1964) investigation. When the loss of both parents included the death of one, these subjects scored higher on measures designed to assess their preoccupation with loss. The subjects who had lost both parents were living in orphanages and, therefore, had quite different experiences from the subjects of other studies reviewed.

Parish and Copeland (1980) found that college males who had been paternally bereaved were more externally oriented than were paternally bereaved females and individuals of both sexes with divorced parents and intact families. Such a finding would not be unexpected, since the parents of the nonbereaved subjects clearly had more control over their lives. The sex difference on this variable is not easily explained.

The other level-II study on personality conducted by Santrock and Wohlford (1970) showed that ten-year-old boys who were father absent due to death had less trouble delaying gratification than boys whose parents were divorced. The bereaved subjects were also less aggressive. These findings are consistent with those of Felner, Stolberg and Cowen (1975), showing that parentally bereaved children tend to be more controlled and passive than children of divorced parents, and to behave in a manner that seems more socially acceptable.

Three methodologically sound studies concerned with sex-role functioning and social behavior with members of the other sex also had outcomes similar to those obtained by Santrock and Wohlford and Felner, Stolberg, and Cowen. Clarke (1971), in his study of father-absent boys, found a substantial disturbance in masculine identification in subjects who were bereaved or permanently separated from their fathers. Boys whose parents were separated or divorced and therefore experienced only intermittant father absence had fewer problems with masculine identification. A more passive, dependent style of behavior might be expected from boys less identified with the male role. Hetherington (1972) found daughters of divorcées aggressive and seeking attention from males, while the daughters of widows were shy and avoided physical proximity with males. Hainline and Feig (1978), using older and higher social class subjects, failed to find results consistent with Hetherington's in their replication of her study. They found no differences between children of widows and divorcées.

Data on marital relationships have been inconsistent with studies showing that bereaved children tend towards passive conformity, while children who have divorced parents are more likely to act-out. Hetherington and Parke (1979, citing findings of a study by Hetherington, Cox, and Cox 1978) discovered that women whose parents were divorced were likely to have married young and to have been pregnant at the time of their marriage, to have husbands with criminal records, problems with impulse control, and to have had marital difficulties resulting in separation or divorce. In contrast, women whose fathers had died tended to have intact marriages with ambitious, vocationally successful and socially inhibited men. In Illsley and Thompson's (1961) study, women from homes in which a parent was lost for reasons other than death also more often conceived or delivered children in their teens or before marriage and, like their husbands, were likely to have left school at an early age. Among the bereaved, only those raised by their mother and a stepfather showed similar patterns of behavior, while others who had had a parent die did not differ from women from intact families.

Thus, the popularly accepted notion of differential effects of divorce and bereavement has received some support from empirical studies. Children of divorce, compared to those from intact families and families in which a parent has died, tend to be aggressive, to have difficulty delaying gratification, to act-out and otherwise call attention to themselves. They are more likely to become pregnant out of wedlock and to have unsatisfactory marriages, possibly due to impulsiveness. They may perform poorly on cognitive and achievement tests. In contrast, individuals who have lost a parent to death show less assertive behaviors; they are withdrawn, anxious, depressed, and less likely to have the cognitive, academic, impulse-control, and marital problems seen in children of divorced parents.

Reason for Death

The reason for a parent's absence can be specified beyond distinguishing between death and other forms of loss, and it would seem that these differentiations would be important in understanding a child's subsequent behaviors. Death can result from sudden or prolonged illness, which may or may not be genetically linked, from an accident, suicide, homicide, or from military-related causes. Each of these forms of death carries with it certain psycho-social implications. The family of a suicide or homicide victim may be stigmatized, while a military-related death may reflect honor on surviving family members. Death of a parent from an illness with a genetic basis may lead to excessive concern about one's own health. Despite these potentially different effects of various forms of death, this subject has been considered to a very minimal extent by researchers. The literature is comprised of two empirical studies on surviving children of suicide victims, several case studies and theoretical articles on families in which a suicide has taken place, one article describing a number of families in which a homicide occurred, and two theoretical articles contrasting reactions to sudden and anticipated deaths. This work is reviewed in the following section.

At the most general level, reasons for death can be differentiated as either anticipated or unexpected. With only a prolonged illness would the death be consciously anticipated, although the likelihood of the occurence of each of the other forms of death can, to greater or lesser degrees, be predicted. The family of a military officer, a careless driver, a chronically depressed individual, an alcoholic, or a person involved in criminal activity lives with the knowledge that death may occur prematurely. Yet it is only with a relatively prolonged illness that families are overtly involved in planning for the death. Goldberg (1973) has termed this *anticipatory grief*. Family reactions to such a death are, compared to reactions to a sudden death, more gradual, less intense, and of longer duration. Ideally this process includes the dying person, resulting in an experience of sharing that contrasts with the isolation often felt during bereavement from other causes.

Another level at which forms of death can be differentiated is intentionality. Although this is a relative concept (risk takers may be perceived as contributing to their own deaths), only suicide is clearly intentional. Dorpat (1972) has pointed out that intentional deaths may be perceived of by a child as within the control of both the parent and the child, thereby increasing the likelihood of guilt on the part of the surviving child. Suicide is the one form of death that has been explored, at least clinically, in some detail. Several case studies (by Dorpat 1972; Ilan 1973; Rudestam 1977; Warren 1972) have agreed that suicide of a parent has traumatic effects on surviving children. These case studies have all originated in clinical situations, resulting in a sample biased toward manifestations of maladjustment.

The family situations of suicide victims have been described in some detail, and appear to be related to the outcomes. The tendency of adults to hide the facts surrounding the suicide has invariably led to maladaptation in children (Ilan 1973, Warren 1972). In contrast, families with open communication find support from one another and relationships are often strengthened following the suicide (Rudestam 1977, Volman et al. 1971). Dorpat (1972), however, found that among his sample of seventeen psychiatric patients who had survived a parent's suicide, family relationships prior to and subsequent to the death were marked by problems such as marital discord, other suicide attempts, psychosis in one of the parents, and death of the nonsuicidal parent. Again, this sample can hardly be considered random or widely representative.

Among the reactions of children to a parent's death described in the case studies have been psychosomatic and other physical symptoms, guilt, depression, preoccupation with the suicide, arrested development, overidentification with the deceased, and self-destructive behaviors. Observations have been made from a few weeks after the suicide to sixteen or more years later.

The two empirical studies on reactions to suicide were conducted by Shepherd and Barraclough (1976) and Cain and Fast (1965). These studies, which were rated level I and level II respectively, have been described in detail in the section on emotional disturbance and therefore only outcomes will be described here. Shepherd and Barraclough found that about half of the children they assessed could be described as functioning adequately with regard to school performance and psychological adjustment.

Only-children adapted better than did children with siblings. Children whose families had been characterized by marital discord, criminal activity, or mental-health problems prior to the suicide adjusted less well, as did children whose physical living situation was unstable subsequently. Cain and Fast found that survivors of a parent's suicide were overrepresented among those diagnosed as psychotic in a clinic population.

The one study concerned with families of homicide victims (Burgess 1974) was descriptive and theoretical in orientation. Burgess reviewed case studies of six families in which a member was killed, and interviewed five additional families. She described a two-phase syndrome experienced by families of homicide victims: (1) the crisis phase and (2) long-term reorganization. Interestingly, Volmon et al. (1971) decribes a similar process in families in which there is a sudden death for any reason. During the crisis phase, according to Burgess, there are two types of response: ego-oriented (How does the loss affect me?) and victim oriented, marked by questioning, a need to blame someone and to seek revenge, and identification with other victims. During the reorganization phase, new family roles are assumed and there may be an attempt to seek revenge through legal procedures.

Empirical evidence on reactions to death for different reasons is thus sparse, and applicable only to death by suicide. It is assumed that, in all of the studies reviewed previously, subjects whose parents had experienced various forms of death were grouped together without regard for differences on this variable. Longitudinal studies comparing children whose parents died from different causes would be helpful in determining whether the experiences are, in fact, dissimilar in outcome.

Other Family and Situational Variables

A number of other variables may be related to a child's adjustment and development subsequent to a parent's death. Some of these factors include characteristics of the parent such as age; attitude towards dying; relationship with the child; family variables prior and subsequent to the death, including family adjustment, size and structure, religion, ethnic background, and socioeconomic status. Also of potential importance are the preparation of the child for the death, the type of rituals engaged in, and the degree to which the child is involved in these rituals. The role of these variables has been the source of speculation among some of the writers in the field, and has been considered in a few of the empirical studies. Of interest is the fact that, when family-related variables are analyzed in conjunction with behavioral outcome data, they are often found to be of primary importance, perhaps of more significance than the absence of a parent (Biller 1971, 1974, 1981). In the following discussion, hypotheses and evidence concerning the role of family and situational variables will be presented.

Characteristics of the deceased parent, with the exception of sex, have not been considered by many of the writers and researchers concerned with the effects of a parent's death on surviving children. Yet it would seem that knowledge of the parent and the relationships with his/her children would be of great importance in understanding a child's immediate and long-term reactions. A child who has not been especially close to a parent is unlikely to react in the same way to the parent's death as one whose relationship with the parent has been more significant. A child with ambivalent feelings toward a parent before the death may experience more of a sense of responsibility and guilt with regard to the parent's death than a child who had more consistently warm feelings towards the parent. The strength and nature of the parent-child relationship may be an important determinant of the extent to which a child can use the memory of the deceased parent in a positive or negative way later in life.

The parent's attitude towards dying, if the death is anticipated, would also be likely to influence the child's reaction, as would his/her attitude towards death in a more general sense. Kübler-Ross (1975) observed that childhood experience with death as a natural event, accepted with calm and lack of fear by the dying person, is associated with good adjustment towards death in general and one's own death in particular. Similar effects on immediate reactions to death might also be expected.

A parent's age at death may also have an effect on the child's responses to the event and his/her later behavior. The death of a young parent is likely to affect a child's feelings about his/her own mortality. It is possible that a younger parent may be more closely identified with than an older parent and, therefore, the death would have more of an impact on the child. The parent's age at death may also affect the child as an adult. The approach of the age at which a parent died may well be associated with increased concern about an individual's own well-being. Similarly, passing that age may be experienced with a sense of relief.

Information about the functioning of the family system as a whole would seem to be of some importance in assessing the effect a parent's death will have on a child. In the few studies in which this set of variables was considered, it was found to influence children's subsequent adjustment (Cain and Fast 1965; Shepherd and Barraclough 1976; Trunnell 1968). This result was also found in families in which there was a divorce (Hetherington, Cox, and Cox 1978). For example, Shepherd and Barraclough, in their study of children of suicide victims, found that children functioning inadequately five-to-seven years after the suicide had parents who had had marital separations, criminal records, or emotional problems. Children from less troubled backgrounds made more satisfactory adjustments. Trunnell found severe emotional disturbance to be associated with four factors in addition to a father's permanent absence: severe psychopathology in the father (psychosis, alcoholism, or impulse disorder), severe psychopathology in the mother (psychosis or impulse disorder), periods of long absence of the parent prior to the final absence, and an early history of developmental problems in the child. It may be that, in families in which a parent commits suicide, family problems are common and therefore cannot be separated as discrete factors influencing subsequent adjustment. Dorpat (1972) found family relationships to be traumatic before and after a parent's suicide. Marital discord, psychosis in one of the parents, a prior history of suicidal attempts, loss of the nonsuicidal parent, and a long-standing pattern of invoking guilt in family members by the suicide victim were conditions found to be characteristic of the families Dorpat studied.

A healthy family climate and an adequate level of functioning on the part of individual family members may, in contrast, positively influence adjustment to a parent's death (Biller 1971, 1974; Goldberg 1973, Herzog and Sudia 1973). Volman et al. (1971) suggested that, in families that have been open to the expression of feelings of anger, guilt, sadness, and loss, adjustment to death is less difficult than in families not tolerant of such openness. Also important, according to these authors, is the pattern of role assignment within the family. Reorganization of roles is a major task of mourning and is facilitated by prior explicit distribution of roles according to individual skills and needs. Such families have an automatic process allowing roles left vacant to be reassigned. The dysfunction of families in which role reassignment does not take place has been demonstrated by Boss (1977) in her study of missing-in-action fathers. If the deceased individual held a number of roles or served functions that cannot be readily assumed by others, difficulties in adjustment may arise.

The reaction of family members to the death—which may be predicted, at least in part, by previous indications of adjustment—may also contribute to the effect the parent's death will have on a child. Warren (1972) noted that, if family members do not share information and feelings about the death, children are less likely to be able to cope in a healthy manner. Such a pattern of communication (or lack thereof) is likely to be established previously, as observed by Volman et al. (1971).

Goldberg (1973) has proposed that a number of family tasks must be undertaken in order for adequate adjustment to a death to be achieved. These tasks include: (1) someone giving permission for the grief process to proceed; (2) mutual encouragement of the expression of feelings; (3) relinquishment of the memory of the deceased as a force in family activities (rather than continuing to live as if that person were still alive); (4) realignment of roles within and outside the family. The need for role reorganization has been emphasized by Burgess (1974) as well as by Volman et al.

The surviving parent is usually considered the most important family member in influencing the child's subsequent adjustment and development. The role of the now-single parent was addressed in some detail in the section comparing the differential effects of death and divorce. Most writers have focused on the surviving mother, as research has largely been concerned with the loss of the father. It has been suggested that, when a father is absent, the mother-child relationship is magnified in importance (Biller 1971, 1981) and it may be the quality of those interactions, rather than the father's absence, that most strongly influences the child's behavior (Herzog and Sudia 1973, Shinn 1976). The mother's own level of adjustment, the degree to which she is able to assume the father's functions, her level of involvement with the child, and her success in supervising him or her are the variables which have been identified as significant in this regard (Biller 1972, 1974, 1981; Herzog and Sudia 1973; Shinn 1976). Research concerning surviving fathers would be likely to suggest the importance of his performance in these areas as well as in filling roles usually held by mothers.

The influence of siblings, surrogate parents, and extended-family members such as grandparents, aunts, and uncles has seldom been studied, a serious omission according to some reviewers (Biller 1971, 1974, 1981, Herzog and Sudia 1973). Krupp (1972) has written that the presence of the extended family mitigates against the trauma of death, since the family maintains a collective identity and provides alternative sources of support and affection; also its members are able to share the sense of responsibility for the death. Therefore, he sees the trend towards the nuclear family, geographical mobility, freedom of the individual within the family, and extended childhood that encourage a high degree of involvement with a few family members, as likely to cause a death in the family to be more traumatic and disruptive.

The presence of a surrogate parent would be expected to influence a child in either positive or negative ways, depending on the nature of the relationship developed. All of the variables listed as important with regard to the surviving parent might also be of significance with the surrogate parent since his/her skills may complement those of the surviving parent.

Surrogate parents may be either the new spouse of the surviving parent or a member of the extended family who has volunteered to fill some of the roles of the deceased parent, or an individual hired for that purpose. Except in the case of remarriage, mother surrogates are usually more actively sought and found than are father surrogates (Biller 1981). If the household has previously been run along traditional lines with mother as caretaker for the children and home and father as the wage earner, mothers who lose husbands tend to attempt to fill their absent husband's functional role, while fathers seek others to carry out their wives' domestic tasks. Both bereaved mothers and fathers may enlist the help of their older children in household duties. These children have been shown to make a less satisfactory long-term adjustment than their younger siblings who have had fewer family responsibilities (Illsley and Thompson 1961).

There is some evidence that the presence of stepparents may not necessarily benefit children who have lost a parent through death. There may be a tendency to resent an individual who seeks to replace a deceased parent, as was seen in the study by Bowerman and Irish (1962). These researchers found that bereaved children were less likely to satisfactorily adjust to stepparents than were children of divorced parents, since the latter showed less tendency to unfavorably compare the parent's new spouse with their absent parent. Similarly, Illsley and Thompson's (1961) research indicated that children whose mothers remarried showed a less positive long-term adjustment than did other bereaved children. The child's age at the time of introduction of a stepparent may influence the nature of the adjustment. Most research on parent absence has not specified whether any form of parent substitute is present, thereby confusing any interpretation that might be made about either parent absence or the effect of a surrogate parent.

The ability of siblings to fill needs ordinarily met by parents is also worthy of explanation. Some of the research on sibling and sibling-like relationships suggests that bereaved children may well benefit from peer support. One source of evidence comes from a study of six children orphaned before the age of one who lived in a concentration camp and a succession of hostels until they were three years of age (Freud and Burlingham 1944). These children, who had no consistent adult caretakers, appeared to derive a considerable amount of nurturing and care from their small group of peers. They showed a form of separation anxiety when apart and seemed to place the needs of their group members above their own. More recently, Bank and Kahn (1981) as cited by Adams (1981), found a similar case of sibling loyalty and intimacy in natural siblings. Such relationships were seen only in those whose parents were either absent or inadequate when the children were growing up. The authors concluded that, in such cases of family collapse, sibling relationships increase in importance. In studies of father absence, the presence of older brothers has seemed to mitigate against some of the potentially negative consequences of paternal deprivation (Biller 1981).

Socioeconomic status has been shown to be a significant factor in the way father-absent children adjust and develop. Mother absence and parental death, as differentiated from other forms of absence, have not been systematically investigated. In general, it has been found that lower-class children are more negatively affected by father absence than are those from middle-class families (Biller 1974, 1981; Lynn 1974; Shinn 1976). As Lynn has stated, "Father absence handicaps the lower class child more than it does the middle class child. [The loss of the father] adds to the debilitating effects on the child associated with poverty and the impact of some neighborhoods where there is enormous pressure for conformity to gang standards, and where the child is daily confronted with violence, sexual promiscuity, and the sale and use of hard drugs" (p. 255).

In view of these findings, it is unfortunate that father absence is especially common in lower-class families (Biller 1974). The association between poverty and father absence is due to the fact that father separation occurs more frequently in lower-class families and that loss of the father often results in decreased income. The latter may be less likely to affect bereaved families because of death benefits (Herzog and Sudia 1973). It should be noted that father absence, through divorce, is also common in upper-middle-class families compared to those in the middle class.

Religion and ethnicity are also factors that would seem important in the way children are affected by a parent's death. Ethnicity has been explored only in so much as minority-group status has been associated with poverty and, therefore, with especially extreme effects of parent— or at least father—loss. The traditions and support systems associated with different ethnic groups might also be expected to play a role in the outcome of parental bereavement. Similarly, religious beliefs and practices may be influential in both immediate and long-term reactions to a parent's death. Belief in an afterlife or the continued involvement of the deceased in the affairs of the living would be likely to have a continuing effect on a child's feelings about and behavior subsequent to a parent's death. Lack of such a belief system may be associated with a more extreme sense of loss, which in turn might lead to depression or increased dependence.

Integral to the role of religious beliefs and practices are the various rituals associated with death. Krupp (1972) has suggested that the role of ritual is to channel and legitimize the expression of grief, to encourage the emotional support of friends, and to facilitate establishment of new roles. Children have often been excluded from participation in death rites in the belief that they need to be shielded from the harsh realities of death adults have come to face through the use of just such rituals. The validity of the practice of protecting children in this way has not been fully explored, although one study does seem to support it. O'Brien (1979) found that inclusion of fifth and seventh graders in mourning rituals (not necessarily for their parents) led to increased anxiety about death. O'Brien did not specify the nature of the rituals in which these children took part, however. The reaction of a child to having to view the body of the deceased and perhaps being forced to kiss it might differ dramatically from response to inclusion in a closed-casket funeral service. The short- and long-term effects of participation in different forms of ritual might also differ.

A number of characteristics of the family before, during, and following bereavement may therefore be expected to play a part in the effect of a parent's death will have on a child. To the extent that such variables have been accounted for in research, they have greatly added to the clarity and specificity of findings. Further exploration of the roles of such variables can only increase understanding of the way in which parental bereavement during childhood will influence subsequent adjustment and development

Summary of Research on Family and Situational Variables Related to the Death of a Parent

Based on the evidence presented in this section, it can be concluded that family and situational variables related to the death of a parent are associated with subsequent behaviors observed in the child. Wherever such variables have been considered in empirical research, their importance has become clear. Much of the research has failed to take these factors into account, so that general statements about the findings must be interpreted with caution. One of the best-supported outcomes concerns children's reactions to different forms of parent loss. Children of divorced parents have shown a pattern of acting-out and of undercontrolled behavior, while bereaved children tend to be more constricted and socially acceptable in their actions. Specific forms of death have not been differentiated in the majority of studies. Parental suicide does seem to be associated with problems in children and has also been connected with daily difficulties, both before and after its occurrence. A great deal of research has focused specifically on paternal bereavement, which has been associated with emotional disturbance, personality variables, sex-role and related-interpersonal functioning, cognitive functioning, and delinquent behavior. Except in one study on genius, father absence due to death has been related to deficits or problems in these areas. Death of the mother, which has been less frequently studied, possibly because it occurs less often, has been linked only to emotional disturbance. This research does not necessarily indicate differences in the effects of maternal and paternal bereavement, but does seem to show that death of either parent may make a difference in children's subsequent behavior. Other variables that seem to be related to children's adjustment and development subsequent to a parent's death, but have been the topic of fewer investigations, include factors associated with the loss process, other characteristics of the deceased parent (including age, attitude towards dying, and relationship with the child), and family structure and adjustment, especially behavior of the surviving parent, presence and behavior of other family members, predeath family functioning, and socioeconomic status. The demonstrated role of these environmental-context variables suggests that, in research on parental bereavement, subjects cannot be considered a homogeneous group by virtue of their common experience with a parent's death. The need for a multi-dimensional approach to research in this area is clearly indicated.

5 Characteristics of the Child Related to Behavior Subsequent to Parental Bereavement

Differences among children before the death of a parent would necessarily influence interpretations of subsequent behavior. Temperament; emotional adjustment; cognitive level; academic, creative, and athletic skills; social relationships; and conscience development are some of the broad, functional areas that might be expected to affect and be affected by the major crisis and ongoing deprivation that death of a parent may represent. Researchers, while giving attention to later performance and development with respect to these variables, have not considered functioning prior to the parent's death. Thus, it is not known if subject and control groups compared on these factors were originally equivalent and, as a result, if differences can be attributed to bereavement.

Subjects have been differentiated on major attributes, as age and sex, in some of the research. These studies will be analyzed in the following section. Also reviewed will be the literature on the development of the concept of death in children. Subjects' levels of comprehension of death have not been considered in parental-bereavement studies, but data on the development of understanding of death has significance for the interpretation of the results of this research.

Development of Conceptions of Death

A child's level of understanding of the concept of death would seem to be integrally related to the reaction she/he will have to a parent's death. A child who does not fully comprehend the nature of death would not be expected to have the same response as one who is more knowledgeable. The former may, for example, continue to hope for a parent's return, perhaps connecting some aspect of his/her own behavior to the time or likelihood of the parent's reappearance. A child more aware of the characteristics of death might, conversely, become more fatalistic in his/her outlook. Unfortunately, none of the research reviewed attempted to draw a connection between a child's comprehension of death, the death of a parent, and later behaviors on the part of the child. Research of relatively high methodological adequacy has been conducted on the development of conceptions of death. This research is reviewed in order to (1) illustrate the potential importance of determining understanding of death in assessing parentally bereaved children, and (2) provide information of relevance to the discussion of age-related differences in responses to a parent's death, which will be presented in the next section.

Research in this area has varied in approach but has been relatively consistent in terms of its quality as well as in its results. Methodological and outcome data are presented in table 5—1. The studies were evaluated on outcome measures and the makeup of subject and comparison groups. Outcome measures have included structured interviews with children and/or parents, receptive-language tasks, word-definition-and-association tests, projective measures such as drawings, self-report questionnaires, responses to stories, analysis of play behavior, and measurement of latency of reactions and galvanic skin-responses after death-related statements. Measures of cognitive functioning have often been used to supplement these assessment techniques. The instruments have, for the most part, been of demonstrated validity and reliability. Results have been of such consistency that concern about the few relatively unstructured measurement tools becomes less important.

Studies have all utilized cross-sectional methods, comparing children of different ages on the same variables. A longitudinal approach would have insured matching on all relevant variables, lending credibility to statements about age-related changes found in many of the studies. However, care was taken to account for any intragroup differences that might affect outcome. Age and sex were accounted for in all of this research, and cognitive level, socioeconomic status, religion, and parent's education was controlled for to varying degrees. Except for cognitive level, these differences on other variables usually did not alter outcomes.

The development of an understanding of death has been researched in terms of acquisition of a number of components central to the concept. Kastenbaum (1967) has suggested that comprehension of death involves seven distinct ideas: (1) ability to distinguish the self from others; (2) classification of oneself within a category of beings with the attribute of mortality; (3) the inevitability of personal death; (4) the fact that, while some specific causes of death may be evaded, individual control is limited; (5) the notion of an abstract future; (6) the finality of death; and (7) the inclusiveness of separation from the world of living beings that death entails. Portz (1964) has conceptualized death in more general, less personally oriented, terms that represent the aspects examined by most of the researchers. He conceived of comprehending death as mastering the following issues: death as a temporary or permanent change, reversible or irreversible, a natural or a magical event, and the dead as mobile or immobile, and as physically aware of or insensible to control by external constraints. Knowledge of the inevitability of death, which was mentioned

Table 5–1
Methodological and Outcome Data on Research on the Development of the Concept of Death

Reference	Comparison Group	Outcome Measure	Outcome
Alexander and Adlerstein (1959)	Children of 3–10 years male and female	GSR, latency of response	Differential reaction to death related concepts in children of 5 years and above
Anthony (1940)	Disturbed and nondisturbed school age children, male and female, lower-middle class	Interview, word association, play	Average MA of 7–8 in understanding death; C's under 7 showed limited understanding
Anthony (1972)	2–12-year-old children, male and female, lower-middle class	Parent interviews, word definition, story completion	Five stages in concept development identified, and correlation with age
Hornblum (1978)	4–11-year-old children, male and female	Conservation and time tasks, interview	Age and cognitive level predicted understanding of death; 7–8 = x age for grasping concept
Kane (1979)	3–12 year-olds, male and female	Receptive language task; open-ended interview tapping 9 aspects of death conceptualization, coded Rs	No reification; Age and Piagetian-cognitive level predicted sequential development of death concept; Most concept components acquired by age 8. Death experiences accelerated development in Ss less than 6
Koocher (1974)	6–15-year olds of average IQ, middle class, males and females ethnicity accounted for	Open-ended, structured interview	Piagetian stage predicted concept level; disputed Nagy's results on personification
Maurer (1964)	17–19-year-old females	Unstructured essay: "What comes to mind when you think of death?"	The greater the cognitive ability the less the fear; all understood inevitability
Melear (1973)	3–12-year-old males and females	Structured interview on components of death concept	Full understanding achieved most often in Cs 6 and above The greater the understanding the greater the fear
Nagy (1948)	3–10 year old Hungarian males & females, full range of SES, religion, IQ	Word association, drawings, interview	Three age-related stages identified
O'Brien (1979)	First, third, fifth and seventh grade inner-city parochial students	Questionnaire on death information and anxiety	Age-related level of understanding, class related to anxiety, ritual inclusion related to anxiety

Table 5–1 Continued

Reference	Comparison Group	Outcome Measure	Outcome
Swain (1979)	2–16 year olds, randomized on sex, religion, parent education	Coded structured interviews	Age-related concept continuum; concrete understanding shown at 5–7; abstract understanding in teens
White, Elsom, and Prawat (1978)	K–fourth-grade males and females	Conservation task, R's to story	Age and Piagetian stage related to understanding, universality concept present at 6–7; causal connection related to perceived virtue

by Kastenbaum, and death's universality, were also assessed in many of the studies.

Researchers have found that comprehension of death develops in stages related both to age and to the succession of levels of cognitive development identified by Piaget (1958). Piaget's cognitive stages have also been associated with general-age periods.

The sensorimotor period, which extends from birth to approximately two years of age, is characterized by development of coordination of the senses and the understanding of object constancy. According to Kane (1979), all components of the concept of death are either absent or incomplete during this period. However, basic ideas central to more-complex notions related to death develop at this time. Kastenbaum and Costa (1977) have identified the six-month-old's experiments with the concepts of being and nonbeing (peek-a-boo) as the beginning of the discovery of the meaning of death. Mastering separation anxiety would also be an experience relevant to understanding and eventually dealing with death. In this regard, parental bereavement could make a difference, since children with two actively involved parents tend to show separation anxiety less frequently than those with only one primary caretaker (Spelke et al. 1973). While, generally speaking, children of this age and level of cognitive maturity have no knowledge of abstractions, there have been studies showing awareness of concepts of finitude, irreversibility, and cessation of bodily functions as young as sixteen months of age (Kastenbaum and Costa 1977).

Piaget's preoperational state covers the period roughly from two-to-seven-years of age. A number of concepts are acquired during these years, but many skills necessary to an understanding of death are still lacking. Preoperational children can profit from the experiences of others only to a limited extent, and they still have difficulty distinguishing between animate and inanimate objects. Egocentrism and magical thinking are also characteristic of this stage. Thus, children think of death as something that can be evaded or reversed, and as a relative or temporary state (Melear 1973; Nagy 1948; Rochlin 1967). Melear found that those children viewed the dead as having feelings and as functioning biologically. In Nagy's study, children were found to personify death (a "death man") but this finding was inconsistent with most of the other research. Preoperational children consistently recognized and displayed emotional responses to the concept of death (Alexander and Adlerstein 1959; Anthony 1973; Kane 1979; Swain 1979), although understanding was shown to be very limited. Some cognitive and affective comprehension of death was thus displayed.

Children of seven-to-eleven years of age show characteristics of the stage termed *concrete operations* by Piaget. At this stage, children understand notions of classification, can think in terms of specifics, and can consider two aspects of a situation simultaneously. Attainment of concrete operational thinking (often assessed by easily administered conservation tasks), has been consistently shown to relate to comprehension of such aspects of death as universality, finality, inevitability, irreversibility, and understanding of the dead as lacking the biological capacities of the living (Anthony 1940, 1972; Hornblum 1978; Kane 1979; Koocher 1974; Melear 1973; Nagy 1948; O'Brien 1979; White, Elsom, and Pràwat 1978). In the studies in which Piagetian stage was not specifically determined (Anthony 1940, 1972; Melear 1973; Nagy 1948; O'Brien 1979), the attainment of these concepts was identified as occurring during the years marking the beginning or middle of the period.

The formal-operations stage, which begins at about age twelve, involves attainment of skills in abstract reasoning, hypothesis generation, and the ability to consider more than two aspects of a situation simultaneously. It is at this stage that death is fully understood in abstract, reality-based terms (Kane 1979; Kastenbaum 1967; Koocher 1974; Swain 1979). The understanding of death both within the total view of life, and as a concept of personal relevance is developed at this time.

In younger children, six years and below, experiences with death were shown to accelerate the development of understanding of the topic (Kane 1979). Thus children who lose a parent early in life may come to understand the nature of their loss at a level which would not otherwise be expected. However, early comprehension of death has been associated with anxiety about death (Melear 1973). A similar association has been found with preadolescent children who have been included in mourning rituals (O'Brien 1979). Death anxiety has also been associated with lower cognitive ability in adolescent females (Maurer 1964) and with membership in the middle class (O'Brien 1979). Further exploration of the relationship between cognitive and affective factors in understanding death would be useful. It might be speculated, for example, that emotional disturbance would inhibit or distort acquisition of conceptions of death. The ability to understand both death and the affect associated with it will have implications for the effect a parent's death has on a child's adjustment and development.

Child's Age at the Time of Parental Bereavement

The child's age at the time of a parent's death is another variable likely to make a difference in the effects the loss of the parent would have on the subsequent adjustment and development of the child. Children of different ages have different needs for parental involvement, and, therefore, the initiation of a parent's absence during one period of time would not be expected to influence behavior in the same way that an earlier or later separation would. As was seen in the last section, children of different ages also show dissimilar conceptualizations of death, which in turn may affect behavior exhibited following parental bereavement. A relatively small number of studies have considered the specific ages of children at the time of a parent's death. This research is analyzed and integrated with findings of other reviewers about the development of an understanding of death.

All of the studies reviewed for this project were concerned with the death of a parent during childhood. Thus it was stated (or presumed) that the loss occurred some time before the child's eighteenth birthday. Specification of loss beyond this global distinction was seldom made, however. The present analysis is concerned with research in which there were attempts to differentially relate behaviors to the age at which the loss occurred, or when the range of ages at the time of loss was less than a twelve-year time span. Fourteen of the studies, which were concerned with either emotional disturbance, personality variables, cognitive functioning, or marital adjustment, met these standards. Information on outcomes and ratings of these studies can be found in table 5–2.

Half of the fourteen studies were given a rating of I or II. Of these, adult subjects were assessed in three studies and children and adolescents in four studies. These studies dealt with emotional disturbance, personality, and cognitive functioning. Of the seven relatively adequate studies, six indicated that individuals separated from a parent at some point before the age of eight differed from controls (Baggett 1967; Greer 1964; Haworth 1964; Lifshitz 1976; Santrock 1972, and Santrock and Wohlford 1970). The other level-II study (Birtchnell 1970a) found the critical period for parent loss to be ages ten-through-nineteen.

With respect to cognitive functioning, two level-II studies have dem-

Table 5–2
Ratings and Outcomes on Studies Specifying Age at Parent Loss

| Reference | Age Period | | Behavior Measured | Outcome Measure | Outcome | Rating |
	At Loss	At Assessment				
Hill (1969)	Under 10 10–14 15–19	Adulthood	Emotional disturbance	Psychiatric diagnosis suicide attempt	Suicide attempts were more common in depressed women whose fathers had died when the girls were 10–14 and, to a lesser extent, 15–18, compared with other depressed inpatients; men and women bereaved of a mother when under 10 also attempted suicide more often	III
Lester and Beck (1976)	Under 10	Adulthood	Emotional disturbance	Suicide attempt	Loss of both parents before age 10 was associated with suicide attempts after a recent loss in females	V
Hill and Price (1969)	10–14	Adulthood	Emotional disturbance	Psychiatric diagnosis of endogenous versus reactive depression	Bereavement at 10–14 predicted reactive depression in female patients	IV
Birtchnell (1970a)	10–19	Adulthood	Emotional disturbance	Overt behavioral observations	Men and women bereaved of a parent from ages 10–19 were overrepresented among psychiatric admissions who had attempted suicide	II

Table 5–2 Continued

| Reference | Age Period | | Behavior Measured | Outcome Measure | Outcome | Rating |
	At Loss	At Assessment				
Brown, Harris, and Copeland (1977)	Under 11	Adulthood	Emotional disturbance	Psychiatric diagnosis	Loss of a mother by death, separation or divorce before age 11 was associated with depression among female psychiatric patients	III
Jacobson and Ryder (1969)	Under 12	Adulthood	Marital problems, personality	Interview	Death of the husband's father prior to age 12 was associated with a high rate of marital problems with husbands immature, socially incompetent	V
Huttunen and Niskanen (1978)	Prenatal, first year	Adulthood	Emotional disturbance	Psychiatric diagnosis	Subjects whose fathers died prior to their birth were represented in a schizophrenic population in numbers higher than subjects whose fathers died during their first year of life	III
Barry and Lindemann (1960)	Under 2 Under 5	Adulthood	Emotional disturbance	Psychiatric diagnosis clinical interview	Women who were under 5, and especially those under 2 when mothers died were overrepresented among neurotics	III
Santrock (1972)	Under 2 6–9	Adolescence	Cognitive-academic functioning	Stanford Achievement Test, Otis Quick IQ	Adolescents who were paternally bereaved before age 5, and especially before age 2,	II

Study	Age		Measure	Finding	
Santrock and Wohlford (1970)	3–5 6–9	Personality	Gratification on delay task doll play interview	Boys father separated between three and five showed less ability to delay gratification than those who lost a father earlier or later, but gratification delay was more of a problem for boys father separated by divorce than death; scored lower than controls from intact families	II
Greer (1964)	Under 5	Emotional disturbance	Suicide attempt	Overrepresentation of parent loss from *any* cause before the age of 5 among suicidal inpatients, in contrast to nonsuicidal inpatients	II
Haworth (1964)	Under 6	Preoccupation with loss	Rorschach and TAT, with high interrater reliability demonstrated	Children who had lost one or both parents before age 6 showed more concern with loss than controls from intact families	II
Lifshitz (1976)	3–11	Cognitive social perception skills	Bieri test of cognitive complexity, structured observations, teacher ratings	Children who were paternally bereaved before age 7 showed lower cognitive complexity than nonbereaved controls	II
Baggett (1967)	Under 8	Personality	Sentence completion and self-report inventory	Men father-separated before age 8 (through death) were more submissive than those from intact families	I

onstrated the negative consequences of early death of a father. Santrock (1972) showed that adolescent boys whose fathers had died when the children were aged six-through-nine scored lower on intelligence and aptitude tests than did controls from intact families. Earlier separation was even more significant in children of both sexes who were father-separated for other reasons. In Lifshitz's study, children who were paternally bereaved before age seven were found to be deficient on a scale of cognitive complexity compared to nonbereaved subjects.

The three levels-I and -II studies on personality found differences related to age at parent loss on such diverse characteristics as submissiveness, ability to delay gratification, and concern with loss. Baggett (1967) found men who were paternally bereaved before the age of eight were more submissive than controls from intact families. Concern with loss was shown in children studied by Haworth (1964) when one or both parents were lost (for any reason) before the children were six-years old. Santrock and Wohlford showed that boys father-separated by divorce were less able to delay gratification than were bereaved children. Among bereaved subjects, however, those who had lost their fathers when they were between three and five years of age exhibited less of a tendency to delay gratification.

The one study of relative methodological adequacy showing differences specific to death when a child was over eight was concerned with emotional disturbance. Birtchnell's (1970a) study indicated that men and women who were parentally bereaved during the ten-to-nineteen-year age period were overrepresented among psychiatric inpatients who committed suicide. Greer (1964), in contrast, found parent loss (from any cause) before a child reached five to distinguish suicidal and nonsuicidal psychiatric inpatients. In both studies, adult subjects were studied, indicating that parental bereavement may have long-term effects.

The small number of studies on a wide range of topics in which age-at-loss has been differentially related to outcome precludes conclusions about the type of behavior that might be predicted from parent loss at a given age. Failure to differentially relate age-at-loss with age-at-assessment further impedes efforts at interpretation. The research that can be interpreted with relative confidence is consistent in relating less positive behavior with loss of a parent before age seven. It will be recalled that it is only at about age seven or eight, the beginning of the concrete-operations stage, that children begin to understand death in a realistic way. A lack of comprehension of the meaning or significance of death may, therefore, be associated with negative consequences of a parent's death as the only significant form of parent loss. Other reviewers (Biller 1971; Herzog and Sudia 1973; Pedersen 1976) have concluded that early loss of a parent, or at least of a father, for any reason, is more detrimental to development than a later loss. It is therefore probable that, while the understanding of death may be important, other factors related more generally to a parent's absence are significant. The need for nurturance or for a role model may be greater in the early years, for example. It also may be that the presence of the parent for a longer period of time would have already provided the older child a basis for further, more independent development. Children who lose a parent very early in life may thus be deprived of what they need from parents when they need it most, as well as of the accumulation of parent-related experiences from which to draw on later in life.

Sex of the Child

Females

The issue of sex differences in behavior subsequent to a parent's death might be expected to be related to the sex of the deceased parent. It is generally accepted that all children are in need of parental involvement, but that males and females may look to each parent for the fulfillment of different needs. Differences in outcome by sex of deceased parent have been found, and the failure to specify both variables in studies may be one explanation for the failure to find more sex differences in postbereavement behavior. An alternative explanation would be that fathers are most likely to be deceased, and that their absence has similar effects on both males and females. The general deprivation that may be associated with being raised in a one-parent family may also influence male and female children in the same way. The following analysis focuses on studies in which differences in bereaved and nonbereaved subjects were found specifically for females. The studies reviewed include those using only female subjects and studies in which sex differences were found when both males and females were assessed.

Eighteen of the studies had findings linking parental bereavement to the subsequent behavior of females. As can be seen in table 5–3, seven of these studies were rated in categories I and II. All of the areas of functioning previously discussed, with the exception of cognitive performance, were represented in the seventeen studies. Among the higher-level studies, the topics considered included personality variables, marital and heterosexual-social adjustment, and emotional disturbance.

Eleven of the studies were concerned with the family backgrounds of emotionally disturbed women. Such an emphasis can not only be explained by the general research interest and pattern of positive findings on emotional disturbance among the parentally bereaved, but also by the

Table 5–3
Ratings and Outcomes of Studies on Females

Reference	Behavior Measured	Subjects	Outcome Measure	Outcome	Rating
Baggett (1967)	Sex roles	Male and female college students	Sentence completion and self-report inventory	College women were more feminine on a masculinity-femininity scale when they had been parentally bereaved	I
Barry and Lindemann (1960)	Emotional disturbance	Male and female psychiatric inpatients	Psychiatric diagnosis Clinical interview	Death of mother early in life associated with neuroses in females	III
Birtchnell (1966)	Emotional disturbance	Male and female psychiatric	Psychiatric diagnosis	Females bereaved of mother over-represented among severely depressed	III
Birtchnell (1972)	Emotional disturbance	Male and female psychiatric inpatients	Psychiatric diagnosis	Maternal bereavement in females associated with depression	III
Birtchnell (1975)	Personality	Age and sex matched male and female inpatients	MMPI	Women maternally bereaved before 10 found to be more dependent	II
Brown, Harris, and Copeland (1977)	Emotional disturbance	Female psychiatric patients	Psychiatric diagnosis	Loss of either parent associated with higher incidence of psychiatric depression	III
Dennehy (1966)	Emotional disturbance	Male and female psychiatric patients	Psychiatric diagnosis	Females who lost fathers before age 15 had higher than expected rate of depression	III
Dietrich (1979)	Emotional disturbance	Male and female college students	MMPI, TAT, Rosenweig, Picture Frustration, Test, Lester and Temple, Death-Fear Scale	Psychopathologic trends associated with late childhood bereavement in females, although scores less extreme than males	II
Gay and Tonge (1967)	Emotional disturbance	Male and female psychiatric patients	Psychiatric diagnosis	In women, reactive depression associated with paternal bereavement, other neurosis associated with maternal bereavement	IV

Study	Measure	Sample	Method	Findings	Class
Hainline and Feig (1978)	Personality. Interpersonal behavior with males	Adolescent females	Structured interview and observations on subjects from various family backgrounds	ND among groups	II
Hetherington (1972)	Personality. Interpersonal behavior with males	Adolescent females	Structured interviews Observations	Daughters of widow's shy with males. All father absent = dependent	I
Hetherington and Parke (1979)	Marital adjustment	Female young adults	Structured interviews	Daughters of widows married vocationally ambitious, socially constricted men	I
Hill (1969)	Emotional disturbance	Male and female psychiatric inpatients	Psychiatric diagnosis suicide attempt	Suicide attempted more frequently in depressed when losing fathers after 10, mothers before 10	III
Hill and Price (1969)	Emotional disturbance	Male and female psychiatric inpatients	Nontraditional diagnosis	Females bereaved from 10–14 of fathers more often depressed than others	IV
Illsley and Thompson (1961)	Marital adjustment	Maternity hospital patients	Structured interview self-report scales	Women raised by mothers and stepfather had left school earlier, had lower level jobs as did husbands, conceived in teens or outside marriage, ND from controls with other bereaved subjects	I
Koller (1970)	Juvenile delinquency	Delinquent females	Sentencing to training school	Higher general parent loss	IV
Lester and Beck (1976)	Emotional disturbance	Females who had attempted suicide no controls	Suicide attempt	Loss of parent before 10 associated with suicide attempt after a recent loss	V
Roy (1979)	Emotional disturbance	Female gym students	Psychiatric diagnosis	ND on family background between depressed and others	III

fact that women are overrepresented in psychiatric populations (Chesler 1972). Males tend to be overrepresented in groups with emotional and other problems in childhood, and in criminal populations in adulthood. Only one of these studies was rated at level II, and none at level I, primarily because of the reliance on psychiatric diagnoses as measurement tools. Dietrich (1979) found psychopathological scores on a number of scales in college women who had been parentally bereaved in late childhood. These scores were not as extreme as those of the early-bereaved male subjects.

The three methodologically sound studies dealing with personality variables looked at dependency in women. Birtchnell (1975) found that, among male and female psychiatric inpatients, higher scores on the MMPI dependency scales were found for women who had been maternally bereaved before the age of ten. Hetherington (1972) found that daughters of both divorced and widowed women were more dependent on females than were girls from intact families. However, Hainline and Feig (1978) failed to find differences among groups in their replication of Hetherington's study using older subjects of higher socioeconomic status.

Related to the findings on dependency was the one level-I study on sex-role identification in females. Baggett (1967) found parentally bereaved college women to be more traditionally feminine on a masculinity-feminity scale than women from other family backgrounds. The tendency toward dependency found in other studies might be considered consistent with characteristics viewed as feminine.

Marital and social relationships of bereaved females were examined in four studies meeting the standards for levels I and II. In the study described above, Hetherington found that adolescent girls whose fathers had died were shy and anxious in the presence of males, while girls whose parents were divorced were aggressive and sought attention in such situations. Again, Hainline and Feig found no differences between father-absent and father-present college women. With regard to marital functioning, Hetherington's followup on her 1972 study (described in Hetherington and Parke 1979) and Illsley and Thompson's 1961 study revealed different, but not necessarily inconsistent findings. Hetherington found daughters of widows married vocationally ambitious, socially constricted men, in contrast to daughters of divorcees, who married men of lower vocational accomplishments and were more likely to have conceived outside of marriage, to be married at a younger age, and to experience marital difficulties after a short time. Illsley and Thompson (1961) found women separated from a parent for reasons other than death to be similar to the daughters of divorcees in Hetherington's study, except that Illsley and Thompson's subjects did not have early evidence of marital problems. Bereaved subjects raised with a mother and a stepfather were similar to nonbereaved parent-separated subjects. (The mothers of Hetherington's subjects did not remarry.) Other bereaved women did not differ from controls from intact families.

Differences between females who have been parentally bereaved and those from other family backgrounds have thus been found for subjects who have lost either fathers or mothers. The small number of studies focusing on females or finding sex-related differences does not permit generalizations about the potentially dissimilar nature of the experience of losing a mother or a father on girls; this is a topic that might be given more attention. The literature now available does indicate that losing a parent through death affects female children and that these effects are different from those seen in daughters of divorced parents. Daughters of widowed parents appear to develop a dependent, and perhaps a more socially acceptable, style than daughters of divorcees, who tend to be more assertive. As will be demonstrated, similar tendencies have been seen in bereaved males. This evidence and that presented in the next section indicate that there is little data showing sex differences in children's behavior following the death of a parent

Males

In the general parent-absence literature, there has been more emphasis on the subsequent behavior of male, rather than of female, subjects. The interest among researchers in father absence in contrast to mother absence, may be one reason for this pattern, since there is more concern about boys growing up without a father than about girls in this situation (Herzog and Sudia 1973). Studies specifically on bereavement have not been weighted in this direction, as the behavioral effects of parent death on both sexes have been the topic of a nearly equal number of investigations. Where death of the father has been the focus of research, the concern about the effects of paternal absence on boys has been supported. However, studies have also linked behavioral differences with the death of mothers and of either parent. The analysis that follows will deal with studies on male subjects and with investigations (on both sexes) yielding findings specific to males.

Fourteen studies (see table 5–4) in which parental bereavement was linked with subsequent behavior in male children were located. Six of these studies were rated within the top-two categories, representing all of the areas of behavior previously discussed. Parental bereavement in males has thus been associated with a wider range of behaviors than in females in methodologically adequate studies, including delinquency and cognitive-academic functioning, emotional disturbance, personality, and

Table 5–4
Ratings and Outcome Data on Studies of Parentally Bereaved Males

Reference	Behavior Measured	Subjects	Outcome Measure	Outcome	Rating
Archibald et al. (1962)	Emotional disturbance	Male and female psychiatric patients	Psychiatric diagnosis	Males paternally bereaved: masculine identification problems Males maternally bereaved: dependency and hostility problems	III
Clarke (1961)	Sex role	Age matched boys, father separated for various reasons	IT scale	Father separated boys showed less masculinity on the IT scale, especially those with permanent separation or who had been bereaved	II
Dennehy (1966)	Emotional disturbance	Male and female psychiatric patients	Psychiatric diagnosis, case history of attempts	Excess of male depressives lost mothers before 15	III
Dietrich (1979)	Emotional disturbance	Male and female college students from intact & parent absent families	MMPI, TAT, Rosenzweig, Picture Frustration, Lester and Templer, Death Fear	Early childhood loss of parent associated with MMPI scores indicating pathology in males	II
Gay and Tonge (1967)	Emotional disturbance, marital	Male and female psychiatric inpatients	Case history	Reactive depression associated with death of mother in males, other neuroses with loss of father	IV
Glueck and Glueck (1950)	Juvenile delinquency	Male-identified delinquents	Court records	Paternal bereavement, as well as father absence in general, higher than would be expected in delinquents	I
Hilgard and Neuman (1963)	Emotional disturbance	Male and female psychiatric inpatients	Psychiatric diagnosis	Young alcoholic patients differed in maternal or paternal bereavement from others	III

Study	Characteristic	Sample	Measure	Findings	
Hilgard, Neuman and Fisk (1960)	Academic success	Bereaved males	Interview	Men who had lost their fathers during childhood were academically successful	III
Jacobson and Ryder (1969)	Marital adjustment personality	Bereaved males and females	Interview	Marital difficulty, immaturity associated with paternal bereavement in males	V
Martindale (1972)	Emotional disturbance, poetic eminence	Male poets	Listing in *Oxford Anthology of Verse*, Life histories	Psychopathology, cross-sex identification, and parental bereavement found characteristic of eminent poets	V
Moran and Abe (1969)	Sexuality	Male psychiatric inpatients	Psychiatric diagnosis	No difference in family background of homosexuals	III
Parish and Copeland (1980)	Locus of control	Male and female college students	Rotter Internality Externality Scale	Males from father bereaved families were more externally oriented than males or females from divorced and females from bereaved families	II
Santrock (1972)	Cognitive, academic functioning	Junior and senior high school boys	Stanford Achievement Test, Otis Quick IQ	Father absent—lower cognitive and academic scores, less so for bereaved; Ages 6–9 = critical period for bereavement	II
Santrock and Wohlford (1970)	Aggression, gratification delay	Fifth grade boys	Gratification delay task, doll play interview	Father bereaved boys = less aggressive, more able to delay gratification	II

marital and sexual functioning. This pattern is more related to the diversity of topics investigated for each sex, than to results showing sex differences.

One level-II study yielded sex-specific findings in relation to parental bereavement and emotional disturbance. Dietrich's 1979 research on college students, which was discussed with findings on females, showed that male college students bereaved early in childhood showed more indications of disturbance than both men and women from intact families. Less extreme scores on measures of psychopathology were attained by women bereaved later in childhood, but these scores were still significantly higher than those of nonbereaved subjects.

Findings on personality variables have been relatively consistent for both male and female subjects who have been bereaved, showing a passive, dependent personality pattern. Findings specific to males were yielded in studies by Parish and Copeland (1980) and Santrock and Wohlford (1970). Parish and Copeland found that paternally bereaved males had a more external locus of control than did females with dead fathers, and males and females from other family backgrounds. The authors could not explain the sex difference. Santrock and Wohlford's study of boys with absent fathers showed bereaved subjects to be less aggressive and better able to delay gratification than subjects whose parents were divorced. External locus of control, lack of aggressiveness, and the ability to delay gratification are all consistent with the general personality-pattern seen in bereaved children of both sexes. Clarke's study (1961) on sex-role identification might also be considered as support for these findings. Studying male subjects, he found less traditionally masculine identification in father-absent than in father-present boys. Those who were bereaved or permanently separated from their fathers showed especially strong indications of this pattern.

Glueck and Glueck's data (1950) on juvenile delinquency might be viewed as less consistent with the findings presented above. They found that father-absent boys, including those who had been bereaved, were overrepresented among juvenile delinquents. This extreme form of behavior might be viewed as overcompensation in reaction to doubts about masculinity. Also, as has been observed by Biller (1971), father absence without the presence of a mother able to compensate for this loss, may be associated with susceptibility to the indiscriminate influence of gangs. Such behavior would be consistent with a passive-dependent orientation.

Santrock's 1972 study has indicated that there may be some connection between paternal bereavement and cognitive-academic functioning. Studying father-absent boys, he found lower test scores in those father-absent for reasons other than death than in boys who had been bereaved or were from intact families. Bereavement between ages six and nine, when children are in the earlier grades of school, was associated with less adequate performance, however.

Parental bereavement, and especially loss of the father, has thus been associated with a number of behavioral outcomes in boys; however, most of the sex-linked findings have come from studies in which only one sex was studied. The data on both sexes, where similar types of behavior have been studied, have not shown major sex differences. Exploration of a wider range of behaviors in bereaved females could possibly alter these conclusions.

Summary of Research on Characteristics of Child Behavior Following a Parent's Death

The most significant findings resulting from research on characteristics of the child appear to be related to cognitive development and age. It has been demonstrated that comprehension of death is developed in age-related stages. In addition, younger children appear to be more adversely affected by a parent's death than are older children. Whether this finding is due to the inability of younger children to understand death, to their greater need for parental involvement, to the lack of accumulated benefits of being part of a two-parent home, or to a combination of these factors, has yet to be investigated and resolved. The sex of the child seems to make little difference in the effects of parental bereavement, although isolated studies comparing males and females have found some variations. Investigation of a wider range of variables for female subjects, as well as more systematic attempts to explore sex-of-the-child by sex-of-deceased-parent differences are needed before more definitive statements can be made on this issue. Also needed are studies on functioning prior to bereavement on all areas of behavior discussed.

Summary of the Literature Analysis

The preceding literature analysis included consideration of numerous studies concerned with the behavioral correlates in children of loss of a parent through death. Fewer than half of the studies reviewed were found to meet minimal standards of methodological adequacy. Among the studies of relatively sound methodology, almost all were able to demonstrate the existence of differences between parentally bereaved and nonbereaved subjects. These differences were evidenced both a short time after the parent's death and many years later, when the early-bereaved subjects reached adulthood. Long-term longitudinal studies have not been conducted, however, so that statements about duration and changes in intensity of symptoms within the same individuals cannot be made.

Areas of functioning in which dissimilar behaviors have been found in parentally bereaved and nonbereaved subjects include emotional disturbance; personality; sex-role and related behavior; delinquency and criminal activity; and cognitive, academic, and creative performance. These general topics are the only ones that have been explored, and it has seemed that choice of subject matter has been guided by researchers' assumptions about the way in which bereaved children are likely to behave. Most of the findings have related to adverse consequences of parental bereavement, although some conditions that facilitate positive adaptations to a parent's death have been identified. Adjustment of and relationship to the surviving parent is one factor that may be particularly important in the child's subsequent functioning.

Most of the empirical research has been consistent in showing parentally bereaved children to be more submissive, dependent, and introverted, and less aggressive than children from other family backgrounds, including children whose parents were divorced. Sex-role adoption has thus been more feminine or less masculine in these bereaved children. Other specific correlates of parental death seen when bereaved children were compared with those from other family backgrounds have included emotional disturbance; specifically suicidal behavior; general maladjustment; and, to a lesser degree, psychosis; juvenile delinquency and criminal activity; and both deficiencies and superior performance in cognitive, academic, and creative areas. All types of parent loss, not just bereavement have been connected to delinquent and criminal behavior, and to depressed cognitive and academic functioning.

When family and situational variables have been analyzed in conjunction with behavioral-outcome data, they have often been found to be of great significance. The error in inferring causation from parental bereavement to maladaptive behavior based on simple correlational data has thus been demonstrated. Unfortunately, even in the studies that were rated highly in the research analysis above, consideration of family and situational variables has been minimal. Some of the literature on family and situational characteristics that have been associated with behaviors of children subsequent to bereavement include the sex of the parent and the reason for the loss. It has been shown that death of either parent may make a difference in the child's subsequent adjustment and development. Paternal bereavement has been studied in relation to a wider ranger of variables than has death of the mother, perhaps because the former is a more frequent occurrence. Emotional disturbance, personality variables, sex-role and social functioning, juvenile delinquency and criminal activity, and deficits in cognitive-academic functioning have been associated with death of the father. Maternal bereavement has been related to emotional disturbances exclusively. Children of divorced parents have been found to differ from bereaved children in that the latter are less assertive and independent. Other family and situational variables have not been studied extensively enough to permit specific conclusions to be drawn about their significance.

Less thoroughly explored than family and situational characteristics have been factors specific to the individual child. For example, prior functioning on the behavior-outcome variables shown to be related to parental bereavement has seldom been studied. Thus, it is somewhat difficult to determine whether differences in bereaved and nonbereaved subjects are due to changes in behavior following a parent's death, or to differences in prior functioning of subjects in the two groups. It has been shown that children of different ages and levels of cognitive functioning do differ in their comprehension of the concept of death, and that the development of understanding of the concept follows a predictable, age- and Piagetian stage-related pattern. Level of comprehension of death has not been directly related to the consequences of parental bereavement, but it has been shown that children who are under seven when the death occurs, and therefore are less likely to have attained a full understanding of death, adjust less adequately subsequent to bereavement. These children have also suffered a longer period of parental deprivation than children who are older when the death occurs. In addition to age, sex of the child has been studied in relation to potential differences in the effects of a parent's death. No sex differences were found, but this finding may reflect more the minimal exploration of this possibility with regard to a variety of topics than the fact that no differential effects occur. Characteristics of the child should be explored in more detail as it would seem that such variables, along with family and situational factors, would indicate more specifically which children are particularly vulnerable to potentially adverse consequences of a parent's death.

The analysis of the literature has thus demonstrated that parental bereavement may be a significant event in a child's life, one that will result in the individual's behaving in ways that he/she would not if the family were not disrupted in this fashion. The relationship between parental bereavement and subsequent behavior is complex, however. It is not the simple fact of a death having occurred, but rather the variables associated with the loss of the parent as well as characteristics specific to the child, that will predict the child's subsequent adjustment and development.

6 Implications of the Analysis of the Literature

Research Considerations

The foregoing analysis of the literature on the child's adjustment and development following the death of a parent indicates that changes in the nature and course of a child's behavior may result from variables involved in parental bereavement. Emotional adjustment, personality, sex-role-related behavior, antisocial tendencies, cognitive and academic functioning, and creativity are areas that may be influenced by a parent's death and the environmental changes associated with it.

However, many researchers have oversimplified the situation. As has been demonstrated, when multiple environmental, family, and child-specific variables are considered, complex relationships between variations on these factors and behavioral outcomes are seen. A model indicating the range of variables that must be considered is presented in figure 6–1. The model reveals the early stage of development of research in this field. Very few of the potential factors involved in behavioral correlates of parental bereavement have been examined by researchers. That nearly every variable investigated has been shown to be related to outcome should support further efforts in this regard.

Research on additional variables related to parental bereavement should include consideration of potential benefits of what is usually viewed as an unfortunate family background. It has been asserted in previous discussions that the death of a parent may well have favorable effects on the developmental process and on outcome characteristics. A parent who is released from an unhappy marriage through the spouse's death may, as a result, have more time, energy, and resources to devote to his/her child. The death of a parent who has been sexually or physically abusive, rejecting, or merely disinterested may positively influence a child's self-concept and emotional adjustment. Even if the parent's death does actually represent a loss, a child's development could be enhanced. She/he could become, of necessity, more independent and develop superior problem-solving skills. She/he could be prompted to work toward higher achievement in order to better serve the parent's memory. The few studies that have attempted to link parental bereavement with achievement indicate the potential for this line of research.

Also neglected and needed in order to more fully understand how a child is affected by parental bereavement have been longitudinal inquiries. Research following a child, ideally from before a parent's death through adulthood would indicate whether immediate effects will endure, whether they change in nature, and the environmental factors that interact with the outcomes. Bendicksen and Fulton's 1975 work suggests that the intensity of effects may lessen with age.

The most important studies dealing with the effects of divorce on children's personal and social adjustment have been done by Hetherington, Cox, and Cox (1978) and Wallerstein and Kelly (1974, 1975, 1976). These studies highlight the importance of the developmental and family-social-system context in evaluating the influence of divorce and father absence on children. The developmental stage of the child and the length of time that has elapsed since the initial family breakup must be considered in attempting to understand how boys and girls cope with the divorce process (Biller 1981).

Hetherington and her coworkers have carried out a very interesting,

Parent Characteristics

Sex[a]	Personality	Relationship and
Age and life stage	Cognitive level, skills	involvement with
Occupation	Emotional adjustment	child

Family Characteristics

Parent's Marital	Other household	Religion
situation	members	Ethnicity
Siblings: age, ordinal	Quality of interactions[a]	SES[a]
position	Role distribution	Belief system
	Previous family deaths	Residence

Child Characteristics

Sex[a]	Social behavior:	admission, school-
Age[a]	social skills, sex role,	evaluation referral,
Level of understanding	aggression, conscience	court-evaluation
of death	development	referral
Cognitive level,	Personality,	Symptoms of:
disabilities	temperament:	juvenile delinquency,
Academic status	introversion-	character disorder,
Creativity and special	extroversion, locus of	depression,
talents—divergent	control, egocentrism,	hyperkinesis,
thinking, talents in	dependence, maturity,	schizophrenia,
art, music, writing,	self-concept	substance addiction,
scientific research	Emotional and behavior	paranoia, anxiety,
Physical development	problems:	psychosomatic
	clinic/hospital	disorder

Parent Death

Type:	homicide	Degree and type of
illness (sudden,	war related	preparation the child
prolonged, genetically	accidental	is provided
based)	Attitude of dying parent	Rituals and degree to
suicide[a]		which child
		participates

Situational Changes

Reactions of family members (short, long term)[a] Role redistribution	Changes in behavior toward and expectations of the child	Addition of surrogate parent(s)[a] Change in residence, school[a] SES change

Child's Behavior during Childhood

Immediate mourning responses: depression anger denial self-abuse regression positive adaptive behavior[a] Academic status: achievement[a] level of attainment truancy IQ, specific cognitive abilities, learning disability[a] Creativity, special talents: divergent thinking talent in art	music writing[a] scientific research[a] Physical development: health maturity ability Social behavior: social skills friendships sex role[a] conscience development aggression[a] Personality/ temperament: Introversion/ extroversion[a] Focus of control[a] egocentrism dependence[a]	maturity self concept Behavior problems, psychopathology: clinic[a] hospital admission school evaluation[a] court referral[a] Symptoms of: delinquency[a] character disorder hyperkinesis depression[a] schizophrenia[a] substance addiction paranoia anxiety psychosomatic disorder

Behaviors as Adult

Achievement and level of attainment in higher education Creativity, special talents Social-sexual behavior: friendships marital adjustment[a] parenting behavior aggression social skills Physical health, skills Personality, temperament:	introversion- extroversion locus of control egocentrism dependence maturity self-concept Behavior problems, psychopathology: clinic, hospital admissions[a] court referral[a] symptoms of: character disorder,	criminal behavior,[a] depression,[a] schizophrenia,[a] substance addiction, paranoia, anxiety, psychosomatic disorder Career development: level of attainment, choice of field, work record, SES

[a]Association with parental bereavement/outcome has been demonstrated.

Figure 6–1. Predictive Model of Factors Influencing a Child's Adjustment and Development Subsequent to a Parent's Death

exhaustive, and methodologically complex longitudinal-research project on the effects of divorce on young children (Hetherington, Cox, and Cox, 1978). Because this study is so provocative and also much better controlled than other research endeavors relating to parental loss, it is deserving of special consideration. Hetherington, Cox, and Cox presented data on the effects of divorce on families with preschool-age children. They analyzed a vast array of findings garnered from several types of procedures, including measures of social interaction at home and at school, observer, teacher, and peer ratings. Their longitudinal analyses included assessments of individual and family functioning at various periods of time during the first two years after the divorce.

Hetherington, Cox, and Cox presented evidence that clearly indicates that both father absence due to divorce and high family conflict in intact families, are associated with difficulties in the personal and social adjustment of young children. At one year after the divorce, the father-absent children generally were experiencing more interpersonal conflict at school and at home than were children from high-conflict, intact families. Two years after the divorce, however, the father-absent children seemed to be faring better than were the children from high-conflict families. The girls seemed to be less affected by both marital discord and father absence than were the boys.

Data from the Hetherington, Cox, and Cox study also revealed that father absence, or the decreased availability of the father due to divorce, is associated with a lowered level of cognitive and sex-role functioning in boys two years after the divorce. Girls at the same age, however, did not appear to be similarly affected. However, individual differences in the quality of mother-child interactions in the father-absent home had a strong association for both the boys' and girls' cognitive functioning and personal and social adjustment two years after the divorce. It would be interesting to know if similar results would be found when the reason for father absence was due to the father's death rather than divorce.

Wallerstein and Kelly (1974, 1976, 1980a, 1980b) have reported much interesting longitudinal data from their long-term project studying the effects of divorce on children. Their findings are based on extensive interviews with family members and the children's teachers at three intervals: just after the separation, one year later, and again after five years. The parents in the sixty middle-class families who were involved in the study had initially participated in a six-week counseling program aimed at helping them to cope with divorce-related issues.

In order to assess the effects of divorce on children at different developmental levels, Wallerstein and Kelly (1974, 1975, 1976) divided the children into several different groups on the basis of their age at the time of the initial separation. They divided the children into six different age groups: two-to-three-year olds; three-to-four-year olds; five-and-six-year olds; seven-and-eight-year olds; nine-and-ten-year olds, and those from thirteen through eighteen. The youngest children (two-and-three-year olds) were particularly prone to regress and to express bewilderment, anger, and a clinging and indiscriminate neediness toward adults, in reaction to parental divorce. Regression seemed to be rather brief if children received adequate and consistent emotional involvement from adult family members. However, those children who experienced continually intense parental conflict and had mothers who were devastated by the divorce, appeared very depressed and developmentally delayed a year after the divorce (Wallerstein and Kelly 1975).

Among the three- and four-year olds, a poor self-image and loss of self-esteem were frequently concommitant with parental divorce. A feeling of responsibility for the divorce was common among many of the children. More of the five- and six-year olds, in contrast to the younger children, seemed to be able to weather the divorce without manifesting clear-cut developmental setbacks. Such data are, of course, very consistent with other findings indicating that children are particularly vulnerable to early father absence beginning before the age of five (Biller 1971, 1974, 1981).

Children who were seven-to-eight-years old seemed quite depressed in response to parental divorce (Kelly and Wallerstein 1976). They were more likely to show regressive behaviors than were the nine- and ten-year olds, but were more directly communicative about the reasons for their feelings than were the younger children. The seven- and eight-year olds appeared to be frightened about the consequences of the divorce and they all seemed to desperately want their parents back together again, even those who had been exposed to particularly intense and abusive parental conflict. Frequent expressions of sadness about not being with their fathers was especially prevalent for most of the seven- and eight-year olds. A year after the divorce, the modal response seemed to be more a placid resignation than an energetic striving to make the family intact again.

As might be expected from their more mature cognitive development, nine- and ten-year olds often seemed able to deal with divorce in a better controlled and realistic fashion (Wallerstein and Kelly 1976). They were more likely to use a variety of defensive and coping patterns, so that their everyday lives did not seem as disrupted as did those of the younger children. However, loneliness, physical symptoms, feelings of shame, and especially an intense, conscious anger toward the parents was quite common among the nine- and ten-year olds. About half of this age group appeared to cope adequately a year after the divorce, even though they were still dealing with some feelings of sadness and bitterness. In contrast, the other half were severely handicapped by feelings of low self-esteem and depression that often interfered with their peer relationships and academic functioning. Approximately one-fourth of the children were clearly more psychologically disabled one year after the divorce.

For adolescents, the divorce was characterized by much pain, anger, sadness, and often conflicts concerning their parents' sexual behavior (Wallerstein and Kelly 1974). Those adolescents who were relatively mature at the time of the divorce and were able to maintain some distance from their parents' conflicts seemed to be doing better by the end of the first year after the divorce, having developed a strikingly realistic perception of their parents. In contrast, those adolescents who had emotional and social problems before the divorce tended to manifest even more serious difficulties after their parents' divorce.

At the five-year follow-up, many different patterns of adaptation were evident from Wallerstein and Kelly's data (1980a 1980b). In general, about one-third (34 percent) of the children appeared to be doing especially well personally, socially, and educationally. They had very positive self-concepts and showed generally high levels of competence that included coping well with experiences related to the divorce. A slightly greater proportion (37 percent) expressed rather severe adjustment problems including personal and social difficulties, with many having particularly strong feelings of loneliness, alienation, and depression. They were extremely dissatisfied with their lives, though even among this group, about half were able to do adequately in some areas, such as school. The remaining children (29 percent) made what could be termed mixed adjustments, showing typical ups and downs in coping with their life situations. These children appeared to be making an average adaptation to school and social demands, but there was some evidence that feelings about the divorce sometimes had negative effects on their self-esteem and overall competence.

Following a number of groups of children who are bereaved at different ages would similarly expand data on the effects of parental death within a developmental framework. With the techniques applied to children of divorce by Hetherington, Cox, and Cox and Wallerstein and Kelly, initial differences in reactions by children of different ages as well as changes over time could be identified.

In future research, diligent adherence to procedures basic to scientific investigation must be emphasized. Due to failure to employ appropriate comparison groups, insufficient description of subjects and procedures, and inadequate methods of measuring outcome, many of the studies reviewed in this analysis could not be interpreted with confidence. Research utilizing more methodologically sound techniques on hypotheses that have not yet been supported due to these omissions and errors should be encouraged.

Most needed in the field appears to be a study following a large group of parentally bereaved children over time. Subjects would be selected from general parentally bereaved populations, rather than special groups, and would represent a diversity of characteristics with regard to ethnicity, religion, socioeconomic status, sex, age, and intellectual level. This selection process would insure inclusion of subjects from various family backgrounds; family and other situational variables would then be extensively studied. Assessment, ideally prior and subsequent to the parent's death, utilizing standardized instruments, could be conducted with regard to a wide range of abilities, interests, affective tendencies, adjustment, and social and sexual patterns. Long- and short-term effects of parental bereavement could be assessed by following children of different ages through to adulthood. Individual, family, and situational factors that mediate the potential negative effects of parental bereavement could also be determined. Information about children who would be particularly vulnerable following a parent's death would also become evident. Such a large-scale study would undoubtedly yield data that could be applied to programs for prevention and treatment of dissorders related to experiencing a parent's death during childhood.

Treatment Considerations

A number of adverse consequences of parental bereavement have been identified in the literature reviewed, and this data suggests the need for the development of methods for intervention with the bereaved child, his/her family, and the general population. Research on intervention with bereaved subjects has been sparse, with most of the limited literature focusing on proposed treatment approaches and few reports documenting the outcomes of such methods. In this section, implications from the literature on crisis intervention, assessment of the need for longer-term treatment, individual and family therapy, and death education will be presented.

Crisis intervention with the bereaved child would involve preparation for and assistance in dealing with the expected distress the child will experience when faced with the death of a parent. The need for such intervention would be appropriately anticipated by professionals already involved in the children's lives, such as teachers, school counselors, and family physicians (Bascue and Krieger 1974; Berg 1973; Friedman 1968; Hardgrove and Warwick 1974; Hawener and Wallace 1975; Jackson 1973; Jones 1977; and Moller 1967). Some involvement may include dealing with children directly or helping the surviving parent and other family members, and thereby positively affecting the child.

Immediately preceding and following a death, the needs of the child and other family members are for assistance in minimizing the tendency to become overwhelmed and therefore unable to function. The feelings evoked by the family member's death are only a part of the experience with which the bereaved must cope. Funeral arrangements, the notification of family and friends and the dealing with the responses of others to the death are all aspects of bereavement. Crisis intervention should be geared toward helping the family focus on problems one at a time, addressing solvable problems for which practical solutions can be found, before moving on to more complicated issues at the feeling level.

Kirkpatrick (1965) suggested that children should be given complete and accurate information about a parent's impending or recent death. Support for this recommendation comes from a number of case studies documenting the adverse emotional effects of concealing the circumstances surrounding the death (for example, Ilan 1973; Warren 1972). Information about funeral customs and appropriate behavior at different ceremonies should be provided. For instance, a child should be prepared for the presence of an open casket (if it is the custom) and should know how to respond to verbal condolences. Children knowledgeable about death and associated customs, and comfortable with the expectations held for their own behavior, will be better able to handle their feelings of grief.

Encouragement of and assistance in the expression of feelings about the death in the presence of other family members can also be helpful (Paul and Grosser 1965). The purpose of family members' witnessing each others' grief is to decrease guilt for negative feelings and encourage the development of family cohesiveness during the crisis. Facilitation of the expression of emotions may be particularly important for parentally bereaved children, based on the findings of the literature review. It was consistently demonstrated that children who had lost a parent through death showed signs of affective constriction, lack of assertiveness, submissiveness, dependency, and suicidal behavior, which may represent anger turned inward or unexpressed guilt. Assisting parentally bereaved children with the expression of emotions may prevent the development of this pattern of functioning. Intervention at a family level would be most efficient due to the tendency of adults to deny unpleasant thoughts and feelings, especially in the presence of children (Silverman and Englander 1975).

Following the immediate period of crisis, when intervention should be directed primarily at restoring equilibrium (Waldfogel and Gardner 1961), efforts might be directed at helping the child and the family to adjust to their new situation. Help in reorganization of family roles might be required (Burgess 1974; Volman et al. 1971; Warren 1972). Providing support to the surviving parent, who is now in a position to more extensively influence the child, could be indicated (Kirkpatrick 1965). In this regard, encouragement of input from individuals outside the family system could be useful (Klein and Lindemann 1961). If no surrogates for the absent parent are readily available, involvement of extrafamilial members on a long-term basis to fill some of the roles left vacant by the parent's death may benefit the child (Biller 1971, 1974, 1981). As has been mentioned, mother surrogates are more often sought and readily available than father surrogates. The research would indicate that replacement of the father's parental functions would be equally important, however, since both maternal and paternal bereavement seem to have negative consequences for some children. When father surrogates are employed, they are usually for older boys (as the Boy Scouts and Big Brother programs). However, research findings suggest that younger children of both sexes appear to be particularly vulnerable to the effects of the loss of either parent through death, so relevant surrogate programs might be particularly helpful for them.

The need for treatment beyond immediate crisis-intervention can be assessed informally or through evaluation by mental-health professionals. Use can be made of the model for assessing the impact of a parent's death presented in figure 6–1. Those concerned with the child's welfare should, therefore, be aware of interactions among characteristics of the parent, family, and child, the circumstances surrounding the parent's death, and situational changes following bereavement. Special note should be made of changes in the child's emotional, social, cognitive, and academic functioning. Such changes, even if viewed as positive by some family members, may be indicative of a need for mental-health treatment. For example, diminished activity in a child formerly considered overactive may be a reason for concern, possibly related to depression.

Cognitive and projective personality tests can also be used to assess change in a bereaved child, especially if measures of prior performance are available (Bluestein 1978; Shill 1979). Such assessment tools can also be useful in gaining information from children too depressed, withdrawn, cognitively limited, or immature to be verbal about their feelings. It is important to emphasize that responses indicative of disturbance on such tests may well represent a short-term reaction to the parent's death rather than more stable personality traits. The purpose of using these tools should not be for assigning a diagnosis to the child, but rather for identifying children at risk for the development of mental-health problems, and for assessing the appropriateness of psychotherapeutic treatment.

Either individual or family therapy, or a combination of the two may be called for in dealing with a parentally bereaved child. The process of jeopardizing roles may require longer-term family treatment as the more subtle functions the deceased filled in the family become apparent. Expression of feelings in a family setting may not be possible immediately or without assistance, and thus a need for a corrective-mourning experience may be seen (Paul and Grosser 1965). One role a family therapist might play is facilitating acceptance by family members of the different ways in which their grief is expressed. The individual should not have to deal with disapproval of his/her mourning behavior in addition to the already difficult adjustments she/he faces.

Individual psychotherapy for a child may be appropriate for a number of reasons. Many children, especially adolescents, find it difficult to speak openly in the presence of a parent or siblings. This general tendency may be exacerbated in the case of a parentally bereaved child. Children in this situation may be very much aware of the problems of the surviving parent, and thus often hesitant to add to the parent's burden by expressing their own feelings. In addition some children who lose a parent through death tend to become withdrawn, making therapy in a family context even more difficult.

The issues that can emerge in individual therapy with a bereaved child tend to fall into one of three categories: (1) those related to the deceased parent and his/her relationship with the child, (2) those involving the surviving parent and changes in the family, and (3) those regarding the child's feelings about himself/herself. The child is likely to experience guilt in regard to the deceased parent. She/he may feel responsible for the death, believing that something she/he did or failed to do led to or hastened the death. This belief, which is infrequently verbalized outside of the therapeutic situation, is very common. Children also frequently have regrets about the nature of their relationship with the parent, feeling that, had they known they would lose the parent, they would have made more of an effort to get to know the parent or to be kinder. Probably, the most difficult feeling for the bereaved child to handle is his/her anger towards the deceased parent. Anger at the parent for abandoning the child is an expected reaction; in the child's world a parent is a person whose major function is to be there for the child. Unfortunately, a common reaction to a child's anger when the child is open enough to express this feeling, is to deny its validity. ("You don't mean that.") One purpose of therapy is to give permission to the child to experience feelings that may be socially unacceptable and to help him/her to, at the same time, maintain a positive self-concept.

The child's relationship with the surviving parent inevitably undergoes changes following the other parent's death. Many children become concerned about the well-being of the remaining parent, fearing that she/he will die too, leaving the child alone. This fear may manifest itself in a number of ways. The child may refuse to go to school as if, by his/her presence the parent's safety can be assured. The child may take on excessive responsibilities in an effort to spare the parent. An alternative coping-style is for the child to withdraw from the parent to keep himself/

herself from undergoing another loss experience; the child thereby rejects the parent before the parent can leave the child. Another issue involving the remaining parent may be the child's heightened sensibility to his/her needs and problems. The child may refrain from confiding in the parent and strive to protect the parent from unpleasant realities.

Losing a parent through death is also likely to affect a child's self-feelings. The death of a parent often heightens a child's sense of personal vulnerability. Clearly death from a genetically linked illness would be especially damaging in this regard. As has been demonstrated, the experience may affect the child's mood patterns, ideas regarding locus of control, tendencies toward introversion or extroversion, and levels of achievement.

Prevention

Primary prevention techniques would involve education about death in order to decrease the mystery and anxiety surrounding the topic (Hart 1976; Irish 1971; Leviton 1971). Some authors have suggested that this early "immunization" is necessary today because the young have less experience with death due to the segregation of the dying and dead in contemporary life (Irish 1971, Krupp 1972). Perhaps the attitude that has led to our current death-free way of life is the same perspective that has been involved in resistance to death education in schools. Arguments against death-education programs have included: (1) Education about death should be the province of the church and the family; (2) There is no need for death education as death is a natural event and thus is inappropriate for formal instruction; (3) Such a morbid topic is inappropriate for children who should be carefree; (4) Death is a topic only for the elderly who must deal with it directly (Irish 1971, Leviton 1971).

Those who purport that death education is necessary view it as a way of helping children face rather than deny reality. Model programs have included classroom instructions and exploration of feelings raised by death in students as well as parallel education for teachers and parents (Hart 1976; Leviton 1971). Empirical data on stages of development of the concept of death have been used in devising curricula for such programs as well as in texts written for the same purpose (Aradine 1976; Maurer and Muro 1979). Few of these programs have been put into practice, and systematic investigations of those that have been explored are lacking. One researcher who designed a death-education program for preschoolers who had lost a classmate through death did report on the outcome. Berman (1978) found that his subjects improved in their ability to differentiate between separation and death, came to accept death as finite, were more able to express feelings about death, and were less anxious about it. Further research on such programs should be encouraged in order to determine whether they are in fact useful in helping to prepare children for death. In addition, more needs to be known about the nature of the experience of childhood bereavement so that such programs can be developed on the basis of sound theory and empirical evidence. The intuitive notion that preparation for death would benefit children is not a sufficient reason for exposure of groups of students to such programs.

References

Adam, K. Childhood parental loss, suicidal ideation, and suicidal behavior. In E.J. Anthony and C. Loupernik, eds., *The Child in his Family: The Impact of Disease and Death.* New York: John Wiley & Sons, Inc. 1973.

Adams, V. The sibling bond. *Psychology Today.* 15, no. 6 (1981):32–47.

Abrahams, M., and Whitlock, F. Childhood experience and depression. *British Journal of Psychiatry.* 115 (1969):883–888.

Albert, R. Cognitive development and parent loss among the gifted, the exceptionally gifted and the creative. *Psychological Reports.* 29 (1971):19–26.

Alexander, I. and Adlerstein, A. Affective responses to the concept of death in a population of children and early adolescents. *Journal of Genetics and Psychology.* 93 (1959):167–177.

Anthony, E.J. Mourning and psychic loss of the parent. In E.J. Anthony and C. Ksupernik eds, *The Child in his Family· The Impact of Disease and Death.* New York: John Wiley & Sons, Inc. 1972.

Anthony, S. *The Child's Discovery of Death.* London: Kegan, Paul, Trench Traubner, and Co., 1940.

Aradine, C. Books for children about death. *Pediatrics.* 57 (1976):372–378.

Archibald, H.; Bell, D.; Miller, C.; and Tuddenham, P. Bereavement in childhood and adult psychiatric disturbance. *Psychosomatic Medicine.* 4 (1962):343–351.

Baggett, A.T. The effect of early loss of father upon the personality of boys and girls in late adolesence. *Dissertation Abstracts International.* 28(1–B) (1967):356–357.

Bandura, A. and Walters, R. *Social Learning and Personality Development.* New York: Holt, Rinehart, and Winston, 1963.

Bank, S. and Kahn, M. In M. Lamb and B. Suttanmeth, eds. *Sibling Relationships: Their Nature and Significance Across the Lifespan.* In press. Cited in Adams, V. The sibling bond. *Psychology Today.* 15 no. 6 (1981):32–47.

Barry, H. and Lindemann, E. Critical ages for maternal bereavement in psychoneurosis. *Psychosomatic Medicine.* 22 (1960):366–381.

Bascue, L. and Kreiger, G.W. Death as a counseling concern. *Personnel and Guidance Journal,* 52, no. 9 (1974):587–592.

Baumrind, D. Child rearing practices anteceding three patterns of preschool behavior. *Genetic Psychology Monographs.* 78 (1967):43–88.

Beck, A.T.; Sethi, B.B.; and Tuthill, R.H. Childhood bereavement and adult depression. *Archives of General Psychiatry.* 9 (1963):295–302.

Bendikson, R., and Fulton, R. Death and the child: an anterospective test of the childhood bereavement and later behavior disorder hypothesis. *Omega: Journal of Death and Dying,* 6 (1975):45–49.

Benson, L. *Fatherhood. A Sociological Perspective.* New York: Random House, 1968.

Berg, C.D. Cognizance of the death taboo in counseling children. *School Counselor,* 21 no. 1 (1973):28–32.

Berman, D.B. The facilitation of mourning: A preventative mental health approach. *Dissertation Abstracts International.* Ann Arbor, Mich.: University Michigan-Films #78-10684, 1978.

Biller, H. *Father, Child, and Sex Role.* Lexington, Mass.: Lexington Books, D.C. Heath and Company, 1971.

———. The mother-child relationship and the father absent boy's personality development. In U. Bronfenbrenner ed., *Influences on Human Development.* Hinsdale, Ill.: Dryden, 1972.

———. *Paternal Deprivation.* Lexington, Mass.: Lexington Books, D.C. Heath and Company, 1974.

———. Father absence, divorce, and personality development. In M.E. Lamb ed., *The Role of the Father in Child Development.* Second edition. New York: John Wiley and Sons, Inc. 1981.

Birtchnell, J. Depression in relation to early and recent parent death. *British Journal of Psychiatry.* 112, (1966):1035–1042.

———. Relationship between attempted suicide, depression, and parent death. *British Journal of Psychiatry.* 116 (1970a):307–313.

———. Early parent death and mental illness. *British Journal of Psychiatry.* 116 (1970b):281–287.

———. Early parent death and psychiatric diagnosis. *Social Psychiatry* 7 (1972):202–210.

———. The personality characteristics of early bereaved psychiatric patients. *Social Psychiatry* 10 (1975):97–103.

Bluestein, V. Loss of loved ones and the drawing of dead or broken branches on the HTP. *Psychology in the Schools.* 15 (1978):364–366.

Boss, P. A clarification of the concept of psychological father presence in families experiencing ambiguity of boundary. *Journal of Marriage and the Family.* 39 (1977):141–151.

Bowerman, C.E., and Irish, D. Some relationships of step children to their parents. *Marriage and Family Living.* 24 (1962):113–121.

Bowlby, J. Grief and mourning in infancy and early childhood. In R. Eisler ed., *Psychoanalytic Study of the Child.* Vol. 15, New York: International University Press, 1960.

———. Pathological mourning and childhood mourning. *Journal of the American Psychoanalytic Association.* 11 (1963):500–541.

Brill, N., and Liston, E.H., Jr. Parental loss in adults with emotional disorders. *Archives of General Psychiatry.* 14 (1966):307–314.

Brown, F. Depression and childhood bereavement. *Journal of Mental Science.* 107 (1961):754–777.

———. Childhood bereavement and subsequent crime. *British Journal of Psychiatry.* 112 (1966):1043–1048.

Brown, F., and Eppos, P. Childhood bereavement and subsequent psychiatric disorder. *British Journal of Psychiatry.* 112 (1966):1035–1042.

Brown, G.W., and Harris, T. Social origins of depression: A reply. *Psychological Medicine.* 8 (1978):577–588.

Brown G.; Harris, T.; and Copeland, J. Depression and loss. *British Journal of Psychiatry.* 30 (1977):1–18.

Bunch, J.; Barraclough, B.; Nelson, B; and Sainsbury, P. Suicide following bereavement of parents. *Social Psychiatry.* 6, no. 4 (1971):193–199.

Burgess, A.W. Family reaction to homocide. *American Journal of Orthopsychiatry.* 45 (1974):391–396.

Cain, A.C., and Fast, I. Children's disturbed reactions to parent suicide. *American Journal of Orthopsychiatry.* 36 (1965):873–880.

Caplan, G. *Prevention of Mental Disorders in Children.* New York: Basic Books, 1961.

Caplan, M.G., and Douglas, V. Incidence of parental loss in children with depressed mood. *Journal of Child Psychology and Psychiatry and Allied Disciplines.* 10 (1969):225–232.

Chesler, P. *Woman and Madness,* New York: Avon, 1972.

Clarke, P.A. A study of the effect upon boys of father absence in the home. Unpublished doctoral dissertation, University of Maryland, 1961.

Cohen, R. Is dying being worked to death? *American Journal of Psychiatry.* 133 (1976):575–577.

Cox, C. *Genetic Studies of Genius: The Early Mental Traits of 300 Geniuses.* Stanford, Calif.: Stanford University Press, 1926.

Crook, T., and Raskin, A. Association of childhood parental loss with attempted suicide and depression. *Journal of Consulting and Clinical Psychology.* 43 (1975):277.

Crook, T., and Eliot, J. Parental death during childhood and adult depression: A critical review of the literature. *Psychological Bulletin.* 87 (1980):252–259.

Dennehy, C.M. Childhood bereavement and psychiatric illness. *British Journal of Psychiatry. 112 (1966):1049–1069.*

Dietrich, D.R. Psychopathology and death fear. *Dissertation Abstracts*

International. 40 (1979): Ann Arbor Mich.: University Michigan-films #7918593.

Dorpat, T. Psychological effects of parental suicide on surviving children. In A. Cain ed., *Survivors of Suicide.* Springfield, Ill.: Charles Thomas, 1972.

Earle, A. and Earle, B. Early maternal deprivation and later psychiatric illness. *British Journal of Psychiatry,* 109 (1959):181–186.

Eisenstadt, J. Parental loss and genius. *American Psychologist.* 33(1978):211–223.

Epstein, G.; Weitz, L.; Roback, H.; and McKee E. Research on bereavement: A selective and critical review. *Comprehensive Psychiatry.* 16 (1975):537–546.

Felner, R.; Stolberg, A.; and Cowen, E. Crisis events and school mental health referral patterns of young children. *Journal of Consulting and Clinical Psychology.* 43 (1975):305–310.

Ferri, E. Characteristics of motherless families. *British Journal of Social Work.* 3 (1973):91–100.

Fleming, J. The problem of diagnosis in parent loss cases. *Contemporary Psychoanalysis.* 10 (1974):439–451.

Forrest, A., Fraser, R., and Priest, R. Environmental factors in depressive illness. *British Journal of Psychiatry.* 111 (1965):243–253.

Friedman, S. Management of death of a parent or sibling. In M. Green and R. Haggerty, eds., *Ambulatory Pediatrics.* Philadelphia: W.B. Saunders, 1968, 780–783.

Freud, A., and Burlingham, D. *Infants without Families.* New York: International Universities Press, Inc., 1944.

Freud, S. Mourning and Melancholia. In J. Rivers, ed., *Collected Papers of Sigmund Freud.* London: Hogarth, 1950 152–170.

———. *The Ego and the Id.* London: Hogarth, 1961.

———. On narcissim. *The Complete Psychological Works of Sigmund Freud.* London: Hogarth, 1957.

Fulton, R., and Markusen, E. Childhood bereavement and behavior disorders: A critical review. *Omega.* 2 (1971):107–117.

Furman, R. Death and the young child: Some preliminary considerations. *The Psychoanalytic Study of the Child.* 19 (1964):321–333.

———. A child's capacity for mourning. In E.J. Anthony and C. Kouprnik, eds., *The Child in his Family: The Impact of Disease and Death.* New York: John Wiley and Sons, 1973.

Gay, M., and Tonge, W. The late effects of loss of parent in childhood. *British Journal of Psychiatry.* 113 (1967):753–759.

Glass, G. Primary, secondary and meta-analysis of research. *Educational Researcher.* 5 (1976):398–405.

Glueck, S. and Glueck, E. *Unraveling Juvenile Delinquency*. Cambridge: Harvard University Press, 1950.

Goldberg, S. Family tasks and reactions in the crisis of death. *Social Casework*. 54 (1973):398–405.

Granville-Grossman, K. Early bereavement and schizophrenia. *British Journal of Psychiatry*. 112 (1966):1027–1034.

———. The early environment in affective disorder. In A. Cappen and A. Walk, eds., *Recent Developments in Affective Disorders*. London: British Journal of Psychiatry, 1968.

Greer, S. The relationship between parental loss and attempted suicide: A control study. *British Journal of Psychiatry*. 110 (1964):698–705.

———. Parental loss and attempted suicide: A further report. *British Journal of Psychiatry*. 112 (1966):465–470.

Gregory, I. Studies of parental deprivation in psychiatric patients. *American Journal of Psychiatry*. 115 (1958):432–442.

———. Retrospective data concerning childhood loss of a parent. *Archives of General Psychiatry*. 15 (1966):362–367.

Hainline, L., and Feig, E. The correlates of childhood father absence in college aged women. *Child Development*. 49 (1978):37–42.

Hamilton, M. *Father's Influence on Children*. Chicago: Nelson-Hall, 1977.

Hardgrove, C., and Warrick, L.H. How shall we tell the children? *American Journal of Nursing,* 74, no. 3 (1974):448–450.

Hart, E. Death education and mental health. *Journal of School Health*. 56 (1976):407–412.

Hawener, R., and Wallace, P. The grieving child. *School Counselor,* 22, no. 5 (1975):347–352.

Haworth, M. Parental loss in children as reflected in projected responses. *Journal of Projective Techniques*. 28 (1964):31–45.

Heckel, R. The effects of fatherlessness on the pre-adolescent female. *Mental Hygiene*. 47 (1963):69–73.

Herzog, E. and Sudia, C. Children in fatherless homes. In B. Caldwell and H. Ricciuti eds., *Review of Child Development Research*. Chicago: University of Chicago Press, 1973.

Hetherington, E.M. Effects of father absence on personality development in adolescent daughters. *Developmental Psychology*. 7 (1972):313–326.

Hetherington, E.M.; Cox, M.; and Cox, R. Family interaction and the social, emotional, and cognitive development of children following divorce. Paper presented at the Johnson Conference on the Family. Washington, D.C., May 1978.

Hetherington, E., and Deur, J. Effects of father absence on child development. *Young Children*. 26 (1971):233–248.

Hetherington, E., and Parke, R. *Child Psychology: A Contemporary Viewpoint.* Second edition. New York: McGraw-Hill, 1979.

Hilgand, J., and Newman, M. Parental loss by death in childhood as an etiological factor among schizophrenic and alcoholic patients compared with a non-patient Community sample. *Journal of Nervous and Mental Disease* (1963) p. 108.

Hilgard, J.; Newman, M.; and Fisk, F. Strength of adult ego following bereavment. *American Journal of Orthopsychiatry.* 30 (1960):788–798.

Hill, O. The association of childhood bereavement with suicidal attempt in depressive illness. *British Journal of Psychiatry.* 115 (1969):301–304.

Hill, O. and Price, J. Childhood bereavement and adult depression. *British Journal of Psychiatry.* 113 (1969):743–751.

Hoffman, M. Father absence and conscience development. *Developmental Psychology.* 4 (1971):400–406.

Hopkinson, G., and Reed, G.F. Bereavement in childhood and depressive psychosis. *British Journal of Psychiatry.* 112 (1966):459–463.

Hornblum, J. Death concepts in childhood and their relationship to concepts of time and conservation. *Dissertation Abstracts International.* Ann Arbor, Mich.: University Michigan-films #7817306, 1978.

Huttunen, M. and Niskanen, P. Prenatal loss of father and psychiatric disorders. *Archives of General Psychiatry.* 35 (1978):429–431.

Ilan, E. The impact of a father's suicide on his latency son. In E. Anthony and C. Koupernik eds., *The Child in his Family: The Impact of Disease and Death.* New York: John Wiley & Sons. 1973.

Illsley, R., and Thompson, B. Women from broken homes. *Sociological Review.* 9 (1961):27–54.

Irish, D. Death education: Preparation for living. In B. Green and D. Irish. *Death Education: Preparation for Living.* Cambridge, Mass.: Schenkman, 1971.

Jacobson, G., and Ryder, R. Parental loss and some characteristics of the early marriage relationship. *American Journal of Orthopsychiatry.* 39 (1969):779–787.

Jacobson, S., Fasman, J., and DiMascio, A. Deprviation in the childhood of depressed women. *Journal of Nervous and Mental Disease.* 160 (1975):5–14.

Jackson, E.N. Helping children cope with death. In S.S. Cook, ed., *Children and Dying.* New York: Health Sciences Publishing Corporation, 1973, 24–27.

Johnson, M. Sex role learning in the nuclear family. *Child Development.* 34 (1963):319–333.

Jones, W. Death-related grief counseling: The school counselor's responsibility. *School Counselor*. 24, no. 5 (1977):315–320.

Kane, B. Children's concepts of death. *Journal of Genetic Psychology*. 130 (1979):141–153.

Kastenbaum, R. The child's understanding of death: How does it develop? In E. Grollman ed., *Explaining Death to Children*. Boston: Beacon Press, 1967.

Kastenbaum, R. and Costa, P. Psychological perspectives on death. *Annual Review of Psychology*. 28 (1977) 225–249.

Kavanaugh, R. *Facing Death*. Middlesex, UK: Penguin Book, 1972.

Kelly, J.B., and Wallerstein, J.S. The effects of parental divorce: Experiences of the child in early latency. *American Journal of Orthopsychiatry*. 46 (1976):20–32.

Kirkpatrick, J.; Samuels, S.; Jones, H.; and Zweibelson, I. Bereavement and school adjustment. *Journal of School Psychology*. 3 (1965):58–63.

Klein, D., and Lindemann, E. Preventive intervention in individual and family crisis situations. In G. Caplan, ed., *Prevention of Mental Disorders in Children*. New York: Basic Books, 1961.

Kliman, G. Facilitation of Mourning During Childhood. Paper presented at American Orthopsychiatric Association. New York, 1969.

Knobloch, H.; Pasamanick, B.; Harper, P.; and Rider, R. Effect of prematurity on health and growth. *American Journal of Public Health*. 49 (1959):1164.

Koller, K. Parental deprivation, family background, and female delinquency. *British Journal of Psychiatry*. 116 (1970):319–327.

Koocher, G. Talking with children about death. *American Journal of Orthopsychiatry*. 44 (1974):45–52.

Krupp, G. Maladaptive reactions to the death of a family member. *Social Casework*, 53 (1972):425–434.

Kübler-Ross, E. *On Death and Dying*. New York: Macmillan, Inc., 1969.
———. *The Final Stage of Growth*. Englewood Cliffs, N.J.: Prentice-Hall, 1975.

Lamb, M. and Lamb, J. The nature and importance of the father-child relationship. *The Family Coordinator*. 25 (1976):379–386.

Lester, D. and Beck, A. Early loss as a possible sensitizer to later loss in attempted suicides. *Psychological Reports*. 39 (1976):121–122.

Leviton, D. The role of the school in providing death education. In B. Green and D. Irish, eds., *Death Education: Preparation for Living*. Cambridge, Mass: Schenkman, 1971.

Lifshitz, M. Long range effects of father's loss: The cognitive complexity of bereaved children and their school adjustment. *British Journal of Medical Psychology*. 49 (1976):189–197.

Lindemann, E. Symptomatology and management of acute grief. *American Journal of Psychiatry*. 101 (1944):141–148.

Lynn, D. *The Father: His Role in Child Development*. Monterey, Calif.: Brooks/Cole, 1974.

————. Fathers and sex role development. *The Family Coordinator*. 25 (1976):403–409.

McDonald, N. A study of the reactions of nursery school children to the death of a child's mother. In R. Eisler, ed., *Psychoanalytic Study of the Child*. New York: University Press, 1964.

Mace, G.; Akins, F.; and Akins, D. *The Bereaved Child: An Abstracted Bibliography*. New York: Plenum, 1981.

Maher, B. A reader's, writer's, and reviewer's guide to assessing research reports in clinical psychology. *Journal of Genetic Psychology*. 46 (1978):835–838.

Marsella, A., Dubanaski, R., and Mohns, K. The effects of father presence and absence upon maternal attitudes. *The Journal of Genetic Psychology*. 125 (1974):257–263.

Martindale, C. Father's absence, psychopathology, and poetic eminence. *Psychological Reports*. 31 (1972):813–847.

Maurer, A. Adolescent attitudes toward death. *The Journal of Genetic Psychology*. 105 (1964):75–90.

Maurer, C. and Muro, J. Death education: Some issues and suggested practices. *Archives of the Foundation of Thanatology*. 7 no. 66 (1979):

McCandless, B. Children: *Behavior and Development*. New York: Rinehart and Winston, 1967.

Melear, J. Children's conceptions of death. *The Journal of Genetic Psychology*. 123 (1973):359–360.

Miller, Children's reactions to the death of a parent: A review of the psychoanalytic literature. *Journal of the American Psychoanalytic Association*. 19 (1971):697–719.

Moller, S. Death: Handling the subject and affected students in the schools. In E.A. Grollman (ed.), *Explaining Divorce to Children*. Boston: Beacon Press, 1967, 145–178.

Monahan, T.P. Family status and the delinquent child. *Social Forces*. 35 (1957):250–258.

Moran, P. and Abe, K. Parental loss in homosexuals. *British Journal of Psychiatry*. 115 (1969):319–320.

Moriarty, D. *The Loss of Loved Ones: The Effects of Death in the Family on Personality Development*. Springfield, Ill.: Thomas, 1967.

Moss, S. and Moss, M. Separation as a death experience. *Child Psychiatry and Human Development*. 3 (1973):187–194.

Munro, A. Paternal deprivation in depressive patients. *British Journal of Psychiatry*. 112 (1966):443–459.

Munro, A. and Griffiths, A.B. Some psychiatric non-sequelae of childhood bereavement. *British Journal of Psychiatry*. 114 (1968): 305–311.

Murphy, L. Preventive implications of development in the preschool years. In G. Caplan, ed., *Prevention of Mental Disorders in Children*. New York: Basic Books, 1961.

Nagaraja, J. Children's reaction to death. *Child Psychiatry Quarterly*. 10 (1977):24–28.

Nagy, M. The child's theories about death. *Journal of Genetic Psychology*. 73. (1948):3–27.

O'Brien, M. The effects of inclusion and exclusion in mourning rituals on the development of children's conceptual understanding and attitudes about death. *Archives of the Foundation of Thanatology*. 7 (1979):74,

Parish, T., and Copeland T. Locus of control and father loss. *The Journal of Genetic Psychology*. 136 (1980):147–148.

Parkes, C. Recent bereavement as a cause of mental illness. *British Journal of Psychology*. 110 (1964):198–204.

Paul, N. and Grosser, G. Operational mourning and its role in conjoint family therapy. *Community Mental Health Journal*. 1 (1965): 339–345.

Pedersen, F. Does research on children reared in father absent homes yield information on father influence? *Family Coordinator*. 25 (1976):458–464.

Pedersen, F., Rubenstein, J., and Yarrow, L. Infant development in father absent families. *The Journal of Genetic Psychology*. 13 (1979):51–61.

Piaget, J. *The Growth of Logical Thinking from Childhood to Adolescence*. Translated by A. Parsons and S. Seagrin. New York: Basic Books, 1958.

Pitts, F.; Meyer, J.; Brooks, M.; and Winokur, G. Adult psychiatric illness assessed for childhood parental loss and psychological illness in family members. A study of 748 patients and 250 controls. *Annual Journal of Psychiatry*. 24 (1965):121–135.

Portz, A. The meaning of death to children. Unpublished Ph.D. dissertation. University of Michigan, Ann Arbor, 1964.

Price-Bonham, S. Research on roles of fathers. *Family Coordinator*. 25 (1976):489–513.

Quay, H. Classification. In H. Quay and J. Werry (Eds.) *Psychopathological Disorders of Childhood*, New York: John Wiley & Sons, 1979.

Rheingold, H.L. The modification of social responsiveness in institutional babies. *Monographs of the Society for Research in Child Development.* 2 (1956):63.

Richmond, J. and Lipton, E. Studies on mental health of children with specific implications for pediatricians. In G. Caplan, eds., *Prevention of Mental Disorders in Children.* New York: Basic Books, 1961.

Rochlin, G. How younger children view death and themselves. In E. Grollman, ed., *Explaining Death to Children.* Boston: Beacon Press, 1967.

Roe, A. *The Making of a Scientist.* New York: Dodd, Mead, 1953.

Roy, A. Vulnerability factors and depression in women. *British Journal of Psychiatry.* 133 (1978):106–110.

————. Correction to vulnerability and depression in women. *British Journal of Psychiatry.* 134 (1979):552.

Rudestam, K.E. Physical and psychological responses to suicide in the family. *Journal of Consulting and Clinical Psychology.* 45 (1977):162–170.

Santrock, J. Relation of type and onset of father absence to cognitive development. *Child Development.* 43 (1972):455–469.

Santrock, J. and Wohlford, P. Effects of father absence: Influences of, reasons for, and onset of absence. Proceedings of the Seventy-eighth Annual Convention of the APA. 5 (1970):255–266.

Seligman, R. and Glesser, G. The effect of earlier parental loss in adolescence. *Archives of General Psychiatry.* 23 (1974):475–479.

Sethi, B. The relationship of separation to depression. *Archives of General Psychiatry.* 10 (1964):486–496.

Shepherd, D. and Barraclough, G. The aftermath of parental suicide for children. *British Journal of Psychiatry.* 129 (1976):267–276.

Shill, M. TAT measures of core gender identity, parental introjects, and assertiveness in father absent males. *Dissertation Abstracts International,* 39, no. 10B (1979):5087.

Shinn, M. Father absence and children's cognitive development. *Psychological Bulletin.* 85 (1976):295–324.

Silverman, P., and Englander, S. The widow's view of her dependent children. *Omega.* 6 (1975):3–20.

Smith, M. and Glass, G. Meta-analysis of psychotherapy outcome studies. *American Psychologist.* 32 (1977):752–760.

Spelke, E.; Zelazo, P.; Kagan, J.; and Kotelchuck, M. Father interaction and separation protest. *Developmental Psychology.* 7 (1973):83–90.

Spitz, R. Anachtic depression. *Psychoanalytic Study of the Child.* New York: International University, 1946.

Swain, H. Childhood views of death. *Death Education.* 2 (1979): 341–358.

Trunnell, T. The absent father's children's emotional disturbances. *Archives of General Psychiatry*. 19 (1968)::180–188.

Tuckman, J. and Regan, R. Intactness of the home and Behavioral problems in children. *Journal of Child Psychology and Psychiatry*. 7 (1966):225–333.

United States Social Security Administration Statistics. In *Statistical Abstract of the United States*. 100th edition. Washington, D.C.: United States Bureau of the Census, 1979.

Volman, R., Ganzert, A., Picker, L. and Williams, W. Reactions of family systems to sudden and unexpected death. *Omega*. 2 (1971):101–106.

Walton, H.J. Suicidal behavior in depressive illness. *Journal of Mental Science*. 104. (1958):884–891.

Waldfogel, S. and Gardner, G. Intervention in crises as a method of primary prevention. In G. Caplan, ed., *Prevention of Mental Disorders in Children*. New York: Basic Books, 1961.

Wallerstein, J., and Kelly, J.B. The effects of parental divorce: The adolescent experience. In E.J. Anthony and C. Koupernick, eds., *The Child in His Family: Children at Psychiatric Risk*. New York: John Wiley & Sons, 1974.

———. The effects of parental divorce: Experiences of the preschool child. *Journal of the American Academy of Child Psychiatry*. 14 (1975):600–614.

———. The effects of parental divorce: Experiences of the child in later latency. *American Journal of Orthopsychiatry*. 46 (1976):256–269.

———. California's children of divorce. *Psychology Today*. 14 (1980a):67–76.

———. *Surviving the Breakup: How Children Actually Cope with Divorce*. New York: Basic Books, 1980b.

Warren, M. Some psychological sequelae of parental suicide in surviving children. In A. Cain, ed., *Survivors of Suicide*. Springfield, Ill.: Charles Thomas, 1972.

White, E.; Elsom, B.; and Prawat, R. Children's conceptions of death. *Child Development*. 49 (1978):307–310.

Wilson, I.; Alltop, L.; and Buffaloe, W. Parental bereavement in childhood: MMPI profiles in a depressed population. *British Journal of Psychiatry*. 13 (1967):761–764.

Wooton, B. *Social Science and Social Pathology*. London: Allen and Unwit, 1959.

Zilboarg, G. Considerations on suicide in particular reference to that of the young. *American Journal of Orthopsychiatry*. 7 (1937):270–291.

Index of Subjects

Academic achievement, 4, 21,
61–64, 67, 74, 76, 81, 88,
94–95, 97, 114, 115, 126
Addiction, 67, 101
Adolescence, 111, 112, 114, 115,
116, 119, 134
Affiliation. *See* Interpersonal
Relationships
Age of child, 7–8, 20–21, 107–117,
125, 127, 130–134
Age of parent at death, 99, 100
Aggression, 44, 57, 80, 94, 96, 97,
120, 123, 124, 126
Alcoholism. *See* Addiction
Anger, 21, 23, 24, 101, 133, 138
Antisocial behavior. *See* Delinquency
Anxiety, 21, 22, 26, 45, 46, 80, 94,
97
Assertiveness, 44, 45, 80, 97, 121,
136
Attitude of dying parent, 2
Attitude of surviving parent, 91, 99,
100, 102

Behavior problems, 34, 49, 40,
61–64, 98
Belief system, 104
Bereavement process, 19–25
Big Brothers, 137
Boy Scouts, 137
Broken homes. *See* Divorce, Fathers,
Mothers
Brothers. *See* Siblings

Career adjustment, 4, 52, 53, 67,
120
Class differences. *See* Socioeconomic
status
Classroom adjustment. *See* Academic
achievement, School adjustment
Clinic referral, 36, 39, 91, 94
Cognitive functioning, 4, 61–64, 67,
76, 81, 88, 94–95, 97, 112–113,
114, 115, 116, 123, 126, 137

Competence. *See* Cognitive
functioning, Interpersonal
Relationships, Self concept
Conscience development. *See* Moral
development
Courtship. *See* Marital relationships,
Sexual behavior
Creativity, 4, 62–65, 81, 88, 126
Criminal behavior, 2, 3, 27, 42, 56,
58, 60, 67, 72, 81, 84, 88, 97,
101, 120, 126
Cultural deprivation. *See*
Socioeconomic status

Death, concept of, 24, 110–112,
127, 139; different types of, 2,
105, 107–112; reasons for, 95,
97–99, 126
Defenses, 19–25, 33, 136
Delay of gratification, 44, 46, 76,
80, 94, 96, 97, 116, 123, 124
Delinquency, 3, 56, 58–60, 67, 72,
76, 81, 86, 88, 94, 119, 122,
124, 126
Denial, 21, 22, 23, 138
Dependence, 45, 46, 49, 52, 66, 96,
121, 124, 126, 136
Depression, 1, 4, 21, 22, 23, 28, 30,
32, 34, 36, 39, 40, 41, 49, 72,
74, 76, 84, 86, 90, 94, 97, 133,
134, 137
Desertion, 81, 90
Developmental stages, 110–112, 127
Divorce, 8, 44, 45, 57, 81, 90–97,
105, 120, 121, 126, 130–134
Drug addiction. *See* Addiction

Early father absence. *See* Age of
child
Early mother absence. *See* Age of
child
Economic factors. *See*
Socioeconomic status
Education, 130–140

Index of Names

About the Authors

Ellen B. Berlinsky is a psychotherapist at Counseling and Family Services, Inc., a private mental-health clinic in Taunton, Massachusetts. Dr. Berlinsky has had several years of experience providing psychological services at mental-health centers, schools, social-service agencies, residential facilities for the retarded, and health-care agencies. She received the B.A. in 1975 from Syracuse University, the M.A. in 1976 from Columbia University, and the Ph.D. in 1981 from the University of Rhode Island.

Henry B. Biller is professor of psychology at the University of Rhode Island, where he has taught since 1970. He had previously been a faculty member at the University of Massachusetts and George Peabody College, Vanderbilt University. He has been affiliated with a variety of clinical and human-service settings, and is currently a consultant for the group-home programs at the John E. Fogarty Center and the Northern Rhode Island Association for Retarded Citizens. He received the B.A. in 1962 from Brown University and the Ph.D. in 1967 from Duke University. He is a Fellow of the American Psychological Association and is listed in *Who's Who in America*. His numerous publications include *Father, Child, and Sex Role* (Lexington Books, 1971), *Paternal Deprivation* (Lexington Books, 1974), *Father Power* with Dennis Meredith (1974), and *The Other Helpers* with Michael Gershon (Lexington Books, 1977).